Boiling Point

Boiling Point

The High Cost of Unhealthy Anger to Individuals and Society

JANE MIDDELTON-MOZ

Health Communications, Inc.
Deerfield Beach, Florida

www.hci-online.com

A percentage of the author's royalties will be donated to the Confederated Tribes of the Colville Reservation for their new Family Preservation Program. The donation will help provide in-home service to assist in supporting and strengthening families.

Library of Congress Cataloging-in-Publication Data

Middelton-Moz, Jane
    Boiling Point: the high cost of unhealthy anger to individuals and
    society/Jane Middelton-Moz.
        p. cm.
    Includes bibliographical references.
    ISBN 1-55874-668-4 (trade paper)
    1. Anger. 2. Anger—Social aspects. 3. Violence—Psychological aspects.
    4. Aggressiveness (Psychology) I. Title
BF575.A5M5 1999
152.4'7—dc21   98-52014
                                                                     CIP

©1999 Jane Middelton-Moz
ISBN 1-55874-668-4

Publisher: Health Communications, Inc.
             3201 S.W. 15th Street
             Deerfield Beach, FL 33442-8190

Cover illustrations by Lisa Camp

This book is dedicated

to the memory of

Dr. Rudolph I. Moz

and to our family and community

CONTENTS

Acknowledgments ix

Introduction: Living in Emotional Balance 1

1. "I'm Not Angry, but I'm Sick" 21

2. "I'm Not Angry,
   but I'll Get You Back While I Smile" 43

3. "I'm Not Angry, but I Whine and Complain and
   Yes, Indeed, I Blame". 63

4. "I'm Not Angry, but I'm Depressed" 83

5. "I'm Not Angry, but I Sure Will Talk Bad About You". 115

6. "I'm Not Angry, but Get Out of My Way
   on the Highway" 135

7. "I'm Not Angry, but I'm Always Right" 151

8. "I'm Not Angry, but I'm Going to Show *You*
   Who's Boss" 173

9. "I'm Not Angry, but I've Got
   a Lot of Killing to Do" 209

10. Hearing from Our Children 231

11. Achieving Emotional Balance,
    Healthy Values and Strong Communities 245

Appendix: Medications for Effective Treatment of Depression .. 269

Works Cited 275

Index 285

ACKNOWLEDGMENTS

I would like to acknowledge the tremendous support of many individuals during the writing of *Boiling Point*. This book would not have been possible without the time, energy, clinical gifts, heart gifts and generous support of these individuals.

My family: Shawn, Jason, Forrest, Damien and Lisa Middelton; Melinda Moz; Suzy Goodleaf, Diane Labelle and Jamie and Sage Goodleaf Labelle; Ryan and Christopher Flannery; Amy Hinchcliffe; and Alex and Edward Ward for their caring, support, insights and humor, and for just being the people they are.

To Rod Jeffries and Harold and Joy Belmont who stood with Rudy and me throughout Rudy's illness and through the full cycle of seasons following Rudy's death; thank you for your love, strength and prayers.

A special thanks to many members of our community and extended family during one of the most difficult few weeks of my life. Thank you for standing beside our family and holding us up: Ellen Gabriel; Denise David; Della Hill; Vera Manuel; Judalon, Luke, Sam, Jean and John Jeffries; Diane and Bill Laut; Wanda

Gabriel and Paul Ferland; Melissa, Pamela, Katherine and Bernard Gabriel-Ferland; Elaine Lussier; Jimmy, Robin, Jansen and Kyra Nicholas; Christina and Stan Grof; "G." Johnson; Marchetta Davidson; Ann Thompson; Enid LaGesse; Jeff Middelton and Pat Hamerle; Joyce and Willie Nelson; Gina Delmastro, Alex Smith and Angelina Delmastro-Smith; Albert Andrews-Redstar; Veronica Redstar; Kit Wilson; Mary Hansen; Wendy and Kurt Pierson; Frances Brisbane; Lisa Thomas; Anna Latimer; Mary Lee and Denny Zawadski; Mark Adair; David Page; Robert and Sue Barasch; Jonah Meacham; and Mary and Ken Carter.

To Georgine Dellisanti; Jo Ann Chapola; M. MacKay-Brook, Susan Perry, Lee Ann Decker; Rosalyn Rourke, Nancy Broaders, Janyce Vick, for their love, laughter, support and helpful review.

My office manager, Diane Laut, for her competence, caring, laughter and personal support. Behind every successful woman is a successful woman and that's Diane.

A special thank you to Jason Middelton and Ellen Gabriel for their creativity and talent in creating many of the illustrations in *Boiling Point*.

I would like to thank Ruth Crose, Regina Delmastro, Mary Lee Zawadski; Matthew McKay, Peter Rogers, and Judith McKay; Redford Williams and Virginia Williams, for their understanding of physiology that allowed me to create the narrative and cartoons in chapter 1, and Marilyn White and Pat Murtagh for their helpful conversation about communities.

A heartfelt thank you to the third- and fourth-grade class at Rumney School, Angelina Delmastro-Smith, Noel Bishop; Steve Hatcher; Wendy Pierson; Melissa, Bernard and Pamela

Gabriel-Ferland for taking their time to give me their views on violence and anger.

To Christine Belleris for her expert knowledge and editorial support as well as her kindness and compassion; the continued support and caring of Peter Vegso and the staff at Health Communications; and to Ken Carter for his patience and understanding of grammar, as well as his continued caring and friendship.

Also thank you to Diane Labelle for her tireless help with research.

A special thank you to the numerous authors who appear in the Works Cited section of *Boiling Point* and those that have been quoted in the text, for their continued work whose clinical gifts have influenced my thoughts and challenged my mind and heart.

A very special thank you and deep appreciation for my consultees, interns, clients, members of my community workshops and seminars who continually teach me more about the human heart and the strength, compassion and resiliency of the human spirit.

Finally, a special acknowledgment to the countless compassionate, creative and courageous adults and youth that I have met in my travels who continually speak the truth and work hard to strengthen their communities and rebuild a world with a future for our children and grandchildren.

AUTHOR'S NOTE

The individuals and communities mentioned in the case examples are composites of many adults and locales I have worked with in my twenty-nine years of clinical practice. The impact of trauma on individuals and communities is frequently similar. Any similarity of examples to specific individuals or communities is only a result of these common characteristics.

Introduction

Living in Emotional Balance

"Perfection of moral virtue does not wholly take away the passions, but regulates them."

—St. Thomas Aquinas

I travel often. On one particular occasion I was waiting in line to reschedule a flight that had been canceled because of poor weather conditions. The man in front of me was becoming increasingly agitated. He had been muttering to himself, pacing and slapping his tickets against his hand. As the minutes passed, his voice grew louder, "I can't believe these people. This has happened to me one too many times and it's not going to again. They are going to put me on a flight right now, or I'm going to take my business somewhere else! I'm a hundred-thousand-mile flyer, for God's sake."

I thought to myself that his hundred thousand miles in the air weren't going to do him any good if the plane crashed in the middle of the blizzard we were facing. Yet he, and many others like him waiting to be rescheduled that day, appeared not to notice the weather. They seemed to feel the airline was deliberately plotting to ruin their lives.

When he reached the front of the line, the man screamed and hollered, and threatened the ticket agent, who remained incredibly calm and focused. He was still screaming and threatening as he walked away with his rescheduled tickets in hand.

Standing behind me was a mother with three little children. At one point the oldest, who appeared no more than five, asked her mother, "Mommy, why is everyone so angry?" Her mother replied, "I don't know, honey, some people are just angry."

According to news reports, the number of raging passengers is increasing. Federal records indicate that the number of attacks on flight attendants has steadily increased from 296 reported incidents in 1994 to 921 in 1997 (Ken Kaye, Aug. 31, 1998). The cases reported went far beyond this man's verbal abuse. Flight attendants have been physically and emotionally attacked, sometimes in brutal fashion.

Such incidents bring to mind the developing violence in our society. We have "sky rage," "road rage" and "children killing children"; thousands of people are on medication for depression; countless women and children are killed every year in cases of domestic violence; divorce rates remain high. . . . Are some people "just angry," or are we lumping many different reactions and emotions into the category of anger and giving that legitimate emotion a bad reputation?

The gentleman in the airport wasn't expressing healthy anger; he was enraged because he was powerless and out of control. His display of abusive behavior was most likely his common response to frustration. Yet if I asked most people to describe his actions, they would probably say he was angry.

"Anger" is a word that is commonly used to describe a wide range of emotions. Curious how the general public viewed anger, I asked a small number of people for their definitions:

Eleven-year-old boy: *"Anger is a mood and it makes me feel like crying. But it's better to plain get angry than to take your anger out on people or animals. It's not fun being angry."*

Sixteen-year-old girl: *"Anger is a feeling that nobody likes to deal with caused by something that hurts. It's a feeling I fear because when someone's angry, no one knows what they are capable of doing. It is a powerful, uncomfortable and awful feeling and yet we are surrounded by it."*

Twenty-one-year-old student (woman): *"Anger is a feeling that is manifested in many different ways by each person. Some people will lash out at everything and everyone around them, while others will just let it bubble inside and act as if nothing is wrong."*

Twenty-four-year-old snow-making foreman at a ski resort: *"Someone is angry when they have reached or gone past the point of being reasonable—when emotions start to influence thoughts and actions."*

Twenty-seven-year-old restaurant manager (man): *"Absolutely no control over a situation. Feelings of powerlessness."*

Thirty-two-year-old housekeeper (woman): *"Anger is rage inside you that you can't cope with or deal with."*

Given the degree of violence surrounding us every day, it was not surprising that most individuals attempting to define anger actually describe rage.

Anger is a healthy emotion. It is a warning signal that something is wrong. It can alert an individual to the potential for physical or psychological trauma. Anger can provide the energy to resist emotional or physical threats, allowing defense or escape. Anger aids in our awareness of emotional and physical boundaries and helps individuals set healthy limits.

Anger can also mobilize us to make much-needed changes in our world when we are faced with injustices. Consider, for example, Mothers Against Drunk Drivers (MADD), or people who fight for needed legislation regarding child abuse and neglect. Many people who work hard to make the world a healthier place are fueled by anger.

A majority of people in our society appear afraid of healthy anger and are taught from a very young age not to feel it or express it. Many women are socialized to "be nice," not to "make waves," while men are still taught to "fight back" rather than allow themselves to feel normal emotions of vulnerability or powerlessness. Many people are taught not to express feelings at all, while at the same time being systematically desensitized to the violence around them through music, television, movies and video games.

We are a society out of balance. This lack of balance is made apparent in many ways: mentally, emotionally, socially, culturally, spiritually and physically. In forthcoming chapters, I will explore this lack of balance and its dramatic effects on individuals, relationships and society. The effects include symptoms ranging from continual underlying depression and difficulty in relationships to the rage expressed by the airline traveler, as well as many others.

LIFE OUT OF BALANCE

Sages of many cultures have warned repeatedly that "life is out of balance." Nowhere is this lack of balance more noticeable than in the incredible changes that technology has made in our lives since 1950: color televisions take seats of honor in homes throughout the world; video arcades house high-tech games where we can kill almost anything with accompanying sound and lots of blood; guns can shoot seemingly endless rounds of deadly ammunition without reloading; planes, trains and automobiles go faster and faster; technology makes it possible to rebuild many parts of the human body or extend childbearing years into the sixties. Innumerable tasks are performed more efficiently without leaving home by typing "whatever.com" on the computer keyboard. But what of emotions and values? What does all this technological progress have to do with lack of balance and unhealthy anger, especially when progress often saves lives and supports healthy lifestyles?

Our children live in a society that continually uses modern technology to model and glorify violence. Some families are aware of this input and its results. Many people don't allow their children or grandchildren to watch movies that contain senseless violence, play endless rounds of video games that condition violent responses or allow children access to guns, but people often feel overwhelmed and powerless to effect change when so much input into a child's upbringing is provided by influences that the family can't control. Maintaining emotional connectedness and strong values is hard when families have to compete with a consumer culture that has for its support the power of multimillion-dollar marketing campaigns.

Nonetheless, parents and families must work hard to achieve connectedness and build healthy values, for only with a strong foundation will children grow to become healthy adults who can experience a wide range of human emotions, including anger. As mentioned above, properly channeled anger can be healthy for individuals and society. Mishandled or buried anger threatens individuals and society. Becoming competent to deal with and process one's emotions is one of the hallmarks of an emotionally healthy person.

Emotional Competency

From the definitions given for anger earlier, we can see that many people seemed to view rage as anger. Rage is almost always a secondary reaction, resulting from denied feelings of helplessness, frustration, fear, threat, exhaustion or shame. During this age of dual-income families, "Rush! Rush! Rush!" and keeping up with the newest technological "needs" (we rarely say "wants" anymore), the increase in frustration, helplessness, exhaustion and unhealthy expressions of anger should come as no surprise.

Many couples have some of their biggest and least productive arguments on Saturday. I suggest that they are dealing with "re-entry" into the world of couplehood and family. Families rush around and feel so overwhelmed during the week that each person seems to exist within a protective bubble. The major conversations in families during the week often consist of questions: "Did you . . . ?" "Didn't you . . . ?" "Can you . . . ?" "Why can't you . . . ?" In today's busy world, many families do not eat one meal together during the week. Then comes Saturday and family re-entry. Arguments often have underlying themes: "Who are you anyway? Why do you have so little time for me? Why can't you help more so I have a little time to myself? Why am I always so tired and frustrated? It must be your fault."

Emotional competence does not come from hiding feelings or ignoring feelings. Everyone has feelings. Healthy people experience a full range of feelings, from joy to anger to sadness to relief to love. Competence comes in acknowledging these feelings for what they are—feelings—and realizing that they can be expressed in healthy ways rather than denied or used to manipulate, bully or control others.

Most of us as children learned our level of emotional competence from adult models. By five, many of us were taught through observation, physical punishment, or having love and affection withdrawn that anger was not acceptable. One woman told me that her mother used to point to a burned-down house and tell her that if she didn't start controlling her anger that she would burn up like the house. Some individuals, on the other hand, learned to be bullies. They were conditioned to access their anger and to control other people with it in order to get what they wanted. Power and control are often what our children learn from adult models in television, movies and popular music.

Many individuals hide their anger or deny their hostility so effectively that they are not aware of its role in their lives. Anger has ceased to be a healthy, constructive emotion and has become destructive to self and others, as well as to the ability to build healthy relationships. Anger comes out sideways: hurtful humor, clenched jaws, grinding teeth, procrastination, illness, memory loss, chronic lateness, righteousness, gossip, twitching eyes or a constantly moving leg while "relaxing," chronic irritability over small things, depression, or violence.

When we are young we learn by the example of adult models in our lives how to deal with feelings of frustration, helplessness, anxiety, stress and anger. We learn either to pay attention to our bodies and respond appropriately to the messages it gives us or how to ignore our bodies and numb out. We learn to honor and respect ourselves and others or how to look out only for Number One. We gain knowledge concerning what is important to value and what to dismiss as unimportant. We learn balance or how to manage as best as we can without balance.

Violent individuals were often taught when they were young that sadness, vulnerability and powerlessness were too painful or were not acceptable. They learned to bypass vulnerable feelings and go directly into rage. I think of little boys punished for their tears and shamed for expressing sadness, fear or emotional needs by being called "sissies" or "wimps." Such children learn to withdraw kindness, gentleness and caring. Society suffers for these lessons today through escalating youth violence and the loss of young males to jails, institutions and death.

We have become so accustomed to the macho male image that

we sometimes forget that this image is not natural. It is carefully taught to boys at a very early age and continually reinforced by our society. I remember being struck by the natural inclinations of little boys when my husband died. The morning after his death, I was sitting on the back porch crying. My five-year-old nephew came and sat by me on the porch swing.

He put his arms around me and asked, "Auntie, are you sad?"

"Yes, I am," I replied, giving him a hug.

He began gently rocking the chair with his little feet, "Let me rock you gently, Auntie. That always helps me when I'm sad."

Carefully examining from a distance the lives we live, we might find that we need to take several steps back and refocus. Consider a picture of the lives many of us lead. We pursue goals of proving one person right and the other wrong rather than placing value on listening and understanding. We rush to get home five minutes faster, cursing at drivers along the way and putting our health at risk, and when we arrive we use that five minutes we "saved" complaining about one thing or another rather than hugging our children or sitting on the front stoop for a few minutes sharing our day with our significant other.

From a distance, we might see runaway technology without emotional, spiritual or ethical balance. We might see confusion and pain on the faces of children witnessing the adults they love tearing each other down emotionally rather than productively working out differences. We might observe the frustration on the faces of parents trying to do everything alone, and because they do, feeling the loneliness that has been one of their greatest fears. We might see a world where children fear adults and where adults have little idea of how to relate to children. We might see a world where more is better but still never enough. The world we see might be a place where immediate gratification is still too slow and where children kill with little understanding of anger.

Or, after spending time refocusing our energy and taking steps to learn how to be accountable and walk in balance, we might work towards a world of emotional balance. The tenderness and empathy expressed by my five-year-old nephew takes far less energy than a stoic display of non-emotion and is far healthier for the giver and the recipient. So, too, with anger. We need to work toward a world where healthy anger is the norm and destructive anger the exception. Anger is a feeling just like joy or sadness. The actions relating to our anger can be constructive or destructive to ourselves and others, and we can make the choice of which we want them to be. When we make the effort to learn appropriate, healthy ways to understand and deal with our feelings, we can then begin to model those feelings for our children. Then, from one generation to the next, the healing process begins for society.

MODELING IN OUR MODERN AGE

A number of months ago I turned on my computer, clicked my on-line service and checked my e-mail. Among the messages waiting for me was an ad for a super snooper that I could purchase to gather all types of personal information on my "enemies" and one of the more pornographic messages I have read (and I'm not a sheltered individual). I was horrified. *How did these individuals gain access to my personal e-mail?* For me to ask this question was of course ridiculous: Even if I heard the answer,

I wouldn't understand it because I am not one of the most computer-literate people in the world.

My lack of knowledge and the content of the two e-mail messages led me to feel totally helpless and extremely invaded. I tried to block the messages to no avail and then attempted to write a letter to my on-line carrier. I soon found out that with all the time and intellect put into creating this technology, evidently no one had spent an equal amount of time investigating—no one had tried to bring into balance—the emotional, spiritual and cultural implications for our society and especially our children. The focus was merely on the technology, making things easier and quicker with more immediate gratification for our consumer culture.

Two other incidents in the same time period pointed to a similar difficulty with balance: The first occurred during a trip to Oakland, California, where I was giving a presentation. Shortly after we had checked in, my two grown sons, who had accompanied me to the conference, called my room. "Mother, come to our room for a few minutes, there's something you just have to see!" What I just had to see was *The Jerry Springer Show.* None of us watched daytime TV so we weren't up-to-date on what was passing for afternoon entertainment. We were horrified. The show seemed to amount to people screaming at each other about one thing or another and then throwing punches. Much to my disgust I found out that this show's ratings had actually topped other talk shows for three months running. What could consumers be thinking and what would children feel as they watched adults slugging each other on daytime TV? Perhaps the violence was staged, but would children realize that?

Around the same time, an adopted nephew brought me two tapes to view. One was a weekly television show similar to *The Simpsons,* only much more outrageous. *South Park*—one of the most popular shows for middle-school children—has a main character killed in each episode. The one I watched focused on how to kill Grandpa.

The other video he brought, *The Adventures of Little Tom Thumb,* was for even younger children. In one scene, the ogre screams at his wife and squeezes her waist, grabbing her breast in the process. Still screaming, he picks her up, shakes her as if she were a rag doll and throws her across the room. That was enough evidence for me to decide never to watch this particular children's story with my grandchildren.

My nephew wrote a letter to the producers of the video stating that the scenes of domestic violence were not appropriate for little children. He was told that because the ogre was a villain "he was expected to be bad." He was further told that their videos were submitted to a minimum of three, and up to six, classification boards. "In the case of *The Adventures of Little Tom Thumb,* all submissions were returned with a 'G' or General rating." The panel of independent judges, therefore, had contended that the contents of the video fell into the margin of acceptable material for young children. (I wondered if the O. J. Simpson trial would have rated similarly.) I also wondered how the independent panel of judges would feel watching children acting out this particular scene. "I want to be the villain." Later the little "villain" throws the neighbor girl across the room.

Children pay more attention to what's shown to them than to what's said to them countless times. As wise elders are replaced by

TVs and video games, children learn less about healthy emotions and balanced lives. Rather than learning conflict resolution, our children are desensitized to violence and taught to use it as a means of dealing with uncomfortable situations. Operant conditioning techniques used to train soldiers to kill in Vietnam are the same as procedures put to use in many video games.

Many children are being diagnosed with attention deficit disorder (ADD), which in some children has its underpinnings in excessive exposure to out-of-control technology-based "entertainment." I recently spoke with parents whose children had been diagnosed with ADD and placed on Ritalin. I told them, among other things, about recent studies which showed that the choice of recreational activities and diet affects behavior. Excessive television watching and playing of video games leads to a greater incidence of ADD, as do diets that are unbalanced and which contain less than the daily recommended amount of protein. I suggested that parents or other adult caretakers limit children's television time, restrict video games and make certain that they eat plenty of protein in their morning meal.

Some parents listened attentively while I explained the results of several studies and talked about testing for learning-style differences, but when I suggested limiting television and video games and providing well-balanced breakfasts including protein every morning, many resisted: "The only time we have to get things done and spend a bit of time together is when the kids are watching TV or playing their video games." "Maybe we could build in more complete breakfasts on the weekends but the kids love their Pop-Tarts and we don't have time for an argument every morning." "We don't have time to cook breakfast every morning. We're running out the door as it is." A cup of yogurt provides protein, but the target advertising audience for yogurt is not school-age children, so children aren't conditioned to demand yogurt as part of their breakfast. What's more, what do children see their parents eating for breakfast in the morning? What are children's models showing them?

Other parents told me horror stories about being called into schools and told that their children should immediately be put on Ritalin. When the parents asked instead for an evaluation of what might be leading to the hyperactivity, they were put off. Many families spent a great deal of money, time and energy searching for answers and other alternatives. Several of the children had severe learning-style differences. Parents who declined the use of medication were often told that without the medication the child would not change. One woman said that she was told, "You'll see, you'll come back begging us for medication." She didn't. Instead she enrolled her child in a school that focused on children with learning-style differences, paid closer attention to his diet, limited television viewing and more carefully screened her children's TV shows. She said, "It may have taken longer, but my child feels better about himself, more empowered, and won't have to take pills most of his young life." The modeling experience that should be noted here is that a child, no matter how young, can be shown that problems are not always solved with the ingestion of a mood- or mind-altering substance: that through lifestyle and behavioral adjustments, positive change can result. As we'll see later, this approach also gives the child—and the parent—some sense that their own actions play an important role in their lives.

In society today, there seem to be more shortcuts and "conveniences" and less time for quiet walks in the park and meaningful dinner-time conversation. As stated beautifully by Mary Pipher in *The Shelter of Each Other,* we are far too frequently "thirsty in the rain." "Tools have been added to our lives, one at a time, and we haven't been conscious of the psychological effects of all this technology. . . . I'm reminded of a story. A frog who is dropped in a beaker of boiling water will jump out and save himself. But if he is in a beaker with water that's slowly heated, he'll stay in and cook to death. We've experienced change slowly and we haven't jumped." (1996, p. 11)

We can go on-line and communicate with someone in Paris, but can we walk next door and ask for our retired neighbor's help? It truly does "take a village to raise a child," particularly if we want both healthy children and healthy adults.

Even with the conveniences afforded by modern technology and the shrinkage of the world that advancements such as the Internet cause, many of us still can feel disconnected with each other, experience a lack of support and imagine ourselves more and more powerless in a world out of balance. As stated beautifully by an anonymous author in *Changing Community*, edited by Scott Walker:

"When one heard the mason singing on the scaffolding at the top of his voice or the painter whistling (that very curious ability of the lips which seemed to be beneficial to the operation of the paintbrush) it would have been hard to believe that some short decades later these men would be rendered mute and that a transistor radio ever-ready with quick tunes would replace the part that those men gave to sounds of nature. . . . It makes me think of households in which the radio is played and thus people do not listen to their lives." (1993, pp. 30-32)

WORKING TOWARD BALANCE
IN OUR LIVES

Ruth and Sidney stared at me as if I had recently landed on this planet as an alien being: "You want us to *what?*" I had just asked each of them to put a chair in the middle of the room to represent each conflict of theirs that remains unresolved. They now stood on opposite sides of a huge stack of chairs. I asked them if they could see each other, and of course they couldn't. I explained that emotionally this was where they were with each new conflict. As is usually the case, neither had difficulty putting up the chairs. Even with new rules such as speaking only to their own feelings about each incident without blaming the other, this part of the exercise was relatively easy to do.

The rub came when I explained how each chair had to be removed. "In order to remove each chair you must each take equal accountability for why it has remained between you." That's when Jane the alien entered, replacing their previously understanding therapist. They said in unison, "Equal accountability?! But..."

Many of you have picked up this book because you want to read about how a colleague, friend, significant other or child mishandles their anger. Some of you will quietly acknowledge a loved one's particular behaviors and silently validate that you were right about the other's pathology all along. For you to acknowledge your rightness to yourself will be enough. Other readers will only feel justified when they can show the example of unhealthy anger to another, needing the other's acknowledgment and validation that "You were right all along." The readers who will benefit the most from this book will want to learn more about themselves and their world, wanting their own lives to be happier, healthier and more productive. I would suggest that a willingness to "self-explore" rather than "other-blame" is part of the beginning of the work towards emotional balance. It would be useful to make a note of the times that you "other-blame" while reading the upcoming chapters.

Each of us should be aware and accountable for our personal anger triggers—those events that cause us to feel anger. Having triggers is like walking around with a loaded gun inside. Sights, sounds, touch, taste, smells, dates, seasons, holidays and facial expressions—even the ages our children turn—can trigger thoughts and feelings from the past that affect our present responses by causing us to overreact, freeze or underreact. For instance, being stuck in a traffic jam might trigger a feeling of helplessness that was experienced at another time of life. For many, helplessness was a feeling that was not allowed, or that was ridiculed or punished. The helpless feeling is bypassed and the result might be rage.

Working toward balance means first accepting accountability to ourselves, our children, our relationships and finally to our community. For example, if we are suffering from a stress-related illness, it is not the doctor who is going to "fix" us, even with all the technological advances available to medical science. If we are to recover, we must accept accountability for ourselves.

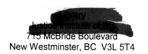

CONNECTION IS A CORRECTION

One of the most important factors in regaining balance is re-establishing connection with our communities. One of the byproducts of isolation and disconnection is increased frustration, stress and vulnerability, resulting in unhealthy expressions of anger. Disconnection is literally killing us.

In an article about school shootings in Oregon, novelist Ken Kesey speaks to community accountability as he describes the tremendous guilt that the adults in the hospital waiting area felt. They may not have had children or grandchildren in the school, but as members of the community they felt accountable anyway: "The waiting room patients and families began to avoid each other's eyes. Where minutes before there had been pride and a kind of narrow strength, now there was an awful dawning: We were guilty of something. It wasn't clear of what just yet, but the guilty expression was unmistakable." (1998, p. 52)

We are accountable to ourselves, our health and our well-being. We are accountable to our children: what we teach about emotional balance and how we teach it. We are substantially accountable for every unresolved conflict in our relationships. And, yes, if we are to begin to reach emotional balance in our communities, we must begin to see ourselves as accountable to each other. Harold Belmont, a trainer and Native American elder, often says, "Prayers are very important, but sometimes we also have to put feet on our prayers."

We can learn about values and accountability to others through the thoughts of children. Ken Kesey relates the thoughts of his granddaughter on the occasion of the Thurston High School murders:

"Why don't they take guns away?"

"Because," I try to explain, "one of the rules in the American rule book says that Americans have the right to own weapons."

"Hmm," she muses. "Then what about bullets? Is there anything in the American rule book that says Americans have the right to own bullets?" (1998, p. 51)

To be mentally, emotionally, physically, socially, culturally and spiritually in balance involves awareness. It means having access to all of our feelings. When we are in balance we are attentive to what our physical selves tell us. Balance means being ethically accountable for the technology that we create and use. Being fully in emotional balance means accountability to ourselves, our children, our relationships and our community. Emotional balance means allowing quiet times and busy times, space to ourselves and time with others. Being balanced means having times when we allow ourselves to need and be taken care of as well as times when we give and take care of others.

One of the most difficult times of my life was after my husband, who was also my best friend, died. After his death, I received many letters asking me if I was angry at God. That feeling never occurred to me. I remember at one time stomping my feet and feeling frustration, helplessness and then anger that Rudy would die and I would miss him desperately. I never felt angry at the Creator, only thankful that I was in the embrace of a loving community. This book has been dedicated to Rudy and to our community. The community that surrounded our family was made up of individuals who encircled us with love and support through death, through one full cycle of seasons of grief—

through life. I found spiritual and emotional balance through being fully supported and loved by each one of these beautiful people and through the beauty that was so clearly around me, even in times of intense emotional pain.

When exploring unhealthy anger it is impossible not to realize the role that a sense of isolation plays in creating lives that are out of balance, and the helplessness, frustration, powerlessness and anxiety that are created by that feeling of isolation. We need each other, yet we seldom truly realize how much.

This book focuses on lives out of balance and the importance of working toward balance in order to experience healthy, constructive anger rather than anger's more destructive counterparts. This book is about working toward emotional, physical, mental, social and cultural awareness. I talk about methods that we can use to be more accountable to ourselves and to develop better communication with each other. Each chapter speaks to the necessity for connection with one another in relationships and in the broader community. The book explores the need to find and maintain healthy balance in our lives.

"I'm Not Angry, but I'm Sick"

"Everything has been figured out except how to live."

—JEAN-PAUL SARTRE

Al had a massive heart attack at age fifty. He was told at the time that 25 percent of his heart was damaged. People often said that Al was such a nice man: quiet, pleasant and easygoing. Some of his employees and his family would describe him differently.

People at work would say that Al was a good boss, easygoing until something went wrong. If an order didn't come in on time, for instance, Al would become agitated. Then he would blow up over a seemingly small incident. Perhaps one of his supervisors would call to let him know that an employee was ill. Al would rant and rave, leaving the supervisor totally confused about what had just happened, because to the supervisor, it wasn't that important.

His wife said that his mood could continue for days. "We would all walk around as if we were walking on eggshells." He would be quiet yet disturbed. When she would ask what was wrong, he would snap, "Nothing." Unfortunately, his son would bear the brunt of his mood. Al would rage at him for the slightest infraction—for leaving a toy outside or not raking the leaves perfectly. Then, suddenly, his mood would leave as fast as it had come. "He'd be all right again and wonder why we were all keeping at a distance."

According to Al's wife, even having fun was serious. "I could tell as soon as he walked into the house how his golf game had gone. If he played badly, he would be in a bad mood for days."

Al is a type A personality. Type A individuals, originally cited in research by Meyer Friedman and Ray Rosenman (1974), are people who are frequently in a hurry, competitive, ambitious, hostile, aggressive and perfectionistic, with a need to be in control and often possessing a cynical outlook on life. According to many researchers, these individuals have high risk factors for illnesses, particularly coronary heart disease. Type A people provide an obvious example of how a personality driven by anger can cause physical deterioration to its host. This chapter looks at the physical effects of anger on one's own body. In addition, the chapter discusses ways to monitor physical signals of anger and how to help correct negative physiological changes caused by anger.

Because type A personalities provide such a clear link between anger and physical illness, studying their actions and the resulting physical changes a little more closely can be instructive. I was able to witness two type A people in action at a party years ago. They clearly demonstrated the personality traits that can eventually lead to chronic hypertension and coronary artery disease. Interestingly enough, they became extremely agitated while engaged in what was supposed to be a leisure activity: attempting to solve the Rubik's Cube puzzle.

For those who may never have encountered a Rubik's Cube, it is a puzzle with six sides. On each side are rows of movable sections with different colors. The object of the puzzle is to move the pieces of the cube in such a way as to make each side a different solid color. It may sound simple but it is quite a complex task. This puzzle proved so difficult for so many people that several books showing techniques for mastering the Rubik's Cube were published.

At a dinner party at a friend's house years ago, one of the guests brought several Rubik's Cubes and handed them out to the other invitees. To everyone's astonishment this individual had actually mastered the puzzle. I have a learning-style difference that makes it difficult for me to master a five-piece jigsaw puzzle, much less a Rubik's Cube. I fiddled with mine for a few minutes and put it down. Several others at the party attempted to accomplish the task to no avail and became temporarily frustrated, but then they waited their turns to learn appropriate techniques from our resident "expert."

Two individuals at the dinner, however, kept struggling with their puzzles throughout the evening. Not only did these two people keep at it as though their lives depended on mastering the puzzle, but early on the task had clearly ceased being fun. They were frustrated; then they became verbally aggressive. One "joked" that the man had brought the puzzles to "show us all up." The other suggested that the puzzle was not solvable and that all of us had been "duped" by the bearer of the gifts. Early into the exercise both individuals began sweating. Their color deepened as their hostility increased. One individual left in a huff. I remember thinking that these two people clearly illustrated the type A personality that I had recently read about. In fact, before turning fifty, one of the two was diagnosed with hypertension while the other developed coronary heart disease.

Observing the two individuals at the dinner party, I could easily see how each had a risk for heart disease. I remember briefly thinking about the movies I had watched in middle-school health classes. Little cartoon characters were used to illustrate how our bodies worked.

Imagine the individuals at the dinner party becoming increasingly stressed as we learn about the physiological effects of anger from the cartoons on the following pages:

As frustration mounts while working the puzzle, a little man living in the left cerebral cortex of each individual picks up a phone and alerts the nerve cells that they need to signal the glands located over the kidneys to pump more adrenaline and cortisol into the bloodstream.

Adrenaline—in the shape of muscular little bodybuilders carrying sledgehammers—begins pounding the heart muscle and forcing it to pump blood faster. As the heart is hammered, the blood pressure rises much like a game at the county fair: A person hits a platform with a sledgehammer, driving a metal device higher and higher until it rings a bell on top of the column.

Meanwhile, a little elderly woman sitting at a computer keyboard in the hypothalamic emergency center in the brain alerts the sympathetic nerves to squeeze tighter in an effort to limit the blood supply to the kidneys, liver, intestines, stomach and skin while the bodybuilders (adrenaline) continue to pump the newly released blood supply to the lungs and muscles, preparing for "fight or flight." The extra cortisol in the bloodstream prolongs the adrenaline's effects on the heart and arteries. (Of course the individuals playing with the Rubik's Cube don't really need this intensified energy flow because they aren't going into "fight" or "flight." They are instead becoming agitated, angry and worked up over a puzzle, but the body doesn't know that. The body thinks there IS an emergency.)

About this time, the cortisol, in the image of a tiny doctor carrying a black bag, fills a tiny hypodermic needle and injects the immune system with a tranquilizing agent, reducing the body's ability to fight infections. This protective measure prohibits the body's highly developed immune system from making antibodies. If a person is physically injured in "fight or flight," it is highly important that he/she doesn't make antibodies in his/her own tissue.

(The individuals with the Rubik's Cubes are not going to be physically attacked while fixating on their puzzles but, again, the body doesn't know that.)

Glucose

Bloodstream

The blood pressure elevates as unhealthy anger increases, and the bodybuilders open bags of glucose and dump them into the bloodstream in order to provide more energy for the impending "fight or flight." Elevated blood pressure will eventually damage the heart muscle. Hypertension forces the heart to work harder and creates a larger and much less efficient heart muscle. An enlarged heart usually indicates that there has been a thickening of muscle tissue. The thick muscle is stiff, creating difficulty in pumping blood effectively. This muscle in its thickened state requires more energy to pump blood, wears out faster, and increases the risk of heart attack and stroke. The heart can also become stretched, baggy and very weak from years of thickened muscle tissue and strain.

Meanwhile, as we imagine the individuals in question becoming more agitated, the body pumps even more blood, producing sweaty palms, deep rapid breathing and more little bodybuilders (adrenaline), who frequently call the operator in the brain to reinforce the message of impending danger.

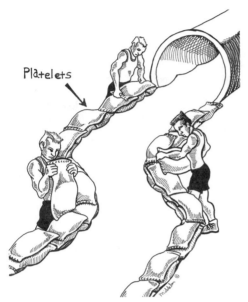

Platelets

The blood rushes faster and faster through the arteries, like a river out of control. Part of the river's edge (coronary artery wall) begins to wear down. Now all of the messengers in the body go on alert. The brain is alerted that there is trouble, and piles of sandbags (platelets) are sent to the location of the damaged river's edge. More and more sandbags are piled up. (Platelets are the cells in the body that cause the blood to clot, protecting an individual from bleeding to death.)

Other blood cells called macrophages (depicted as tiny little scavenger fish) are summoned to eat up injured tissue and other debris.

Macrophages

Platelets release chemical messengers, summoning tiny workers who begin packing thick mud (muscle tissue cells) on the riverbank (artery wall). The mud is packed thicker and thicker in an attempt to repair the riverbank.

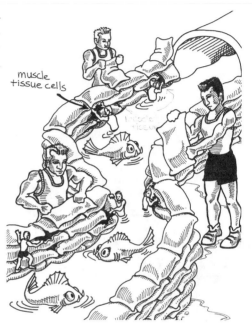

muscle
tissue cells

The bodybuilders (adrenaline) also dump bottles of fat (which the liver turns into cholesterol) into the system as more food supply is needed for the "fight-or-flight" reaction. The fat (cholesterol) ends up being absorbed instead into the sandbags (platelets) and mud (new muscle tissue) because the body doesn't need the extra fat. (The body doesn't need energy; it's going nowhere. It's sitting in one place obsessing over a puzzle.)

With each bout of unhealthy anger, more and more damage is done to the artery wall. With each incident, cholesterol formed from unused fat pours into the bloodstream and accumulates in the platelets and smooth muscle tissue, creating arteriosclerotic plaque ("sludge").

This sludge blocks off the flow of blood into the coronary artery. At some point the plaque will be so thick that it will completely close off the artery, stopping the life-supporting blood to the heart muscle, causing the heart to die piece by piece (the beautiful river will dry up). The individuals who go through the steps just detailed above will develop coronary artery disease, or a clot might form in the blocked artery and travel to the heart, causing a heart attack. These people who place so much importance on solving a puzzle could be two of more than five hundred thousand Americans each year who have a heart attack.

The body is a miracle, obviously created by the greatest technological expert of all time. The Creator was more than an expert in technology. The body is designed to work in balance emotionally, spiritually, mentally and physically and to be in tune with—rather than in opposition to—the environment and creation. The following section of the chapter reviews research regarding anger and health, and what happens when this balance is upended.

A SAMPLING OF IMPORTANT STUDIES

Walter Cannon (1929) found similarities among animals and humans in their response to anxiety and frustration. When Cannon performed autopsies on animals in laboratory studies, he saw the same organ abnormalities—stomach ulcers, enlarged adrenal glands, pale livers, etc.—in all animals, no matter what the type of stress. Of course, these unfortunate animals were subjected to anxiety and frustration by the researchers, unlike humans who frequently bring added anxiety and frustration on themselves due to the way they manage frustration and anger.

A study by Rosenman (1985) found that college students who had hostile personalities were more prone to heart disease twenty-three years later.

Skekelle et al., (1983) collaborated Rosenman's findings in a study of 1,877 people in the Western Electric Company in Chicago. Men who scored higher on hostility tests were one and a half times more likely to have a heart attack than their peers who scored lower on hostility. "Interestingly, the Skekelle study provides some suggestive evidence that hostility may also be related to cancer deaths. In their study, 110 scores were significantly related to a positive direction with twenty-year crude mortality rates caused by malignant neoplasms." (Scheir and Bridges, 1995)

Barefoot, Dahlstrom and Williams (1983) examined the correlation between hostility and coronary artery disease. The study included 255 men who had taken the Minnesota Multiphasic Personality Inventory (MMPI) in medical school. The researchers found that those with hostility scores above the median had nearly five times the incidence of coronary artery disease as those below the median. The researchers were careful to factor out other influences such as age, smoking, alcohol use, etc.

Some studies indicate that indirect venting of anger, such as sarcastic passive-aggressive digs, can be as predictive of heart attacks and coronary artery disease as the direct show of hostility exemplified by the type A personalities mentioned earlier.

Countless research studies cite the contributions of chronic anger to the development of hypertension, ulcerative colitis, digestive problems, ulcers, heart disease, recurrence of genital herpes, susceptibility to infections, headaches, back pain—the list goes on. Much current evidence links chronic anger and hostility to both the development of and morbidity rate of different forms of cancer. (See Works Cited section for listing of research studies.)

Temoshock (1985) proposed that chronically blocked expression of needs and feelings, especially anger (type C personality), resulted in feelings of helplessness under stress, and that helplessness often affected the outcome of cancer. The type C personality, or cancer-prone personality, was originally put forth by Morris and Greer (1975) and described individuals who were emotionally contained. Others have since described type C personalities as individuals who are nice, accommodating, nonassertive, compliant, appeasing and inexpressive of "negative emotions," particularly anger.

Irwin, Anisman and Cox (1984) suggested that anger repression was capable of influencing the neuroendocrine and immune systems in a way that may enhance the appearance of cancer by allowing a small asymptomatic cancer to grow and become symptomatic.

Kune, Kune, Watson and Bahnson (1991) interviewed 637 individuals with confirmed cases of colorectal cancer and 714 control patients, finding that self-reported childhood or adult unhappiness was significantly more common among cancer cases. The frequency of the repression of anger, suppression of reactions and the external appearance of being constantly "nice" as well as avoidance of conflict were found to be significantly higher in cancer cases.

Schacter (1957); Kaplan et al. (1961); Baer et al. (1969); Mann (1977); and Harburg, Blakelock and Roper (1979) performed interesting experiments in which they asked people how they would deal with an angry, arbitrary boss. Some individuals said that they would walk away (anger-in), others said that they would confront the boss and might even report him/her to the union (anger-out). Still another group of individuals stated that they would talk it over later after the boss had cooled down and they had a chance to collect their thoughts. Researchers called this style "reflection." The researchers found that those individuals who used the reflection style had the lowest blood pressure, the anger-out group had the highest, and the anger-in group had slightly lower blood pressure than the anger-out group.

Perhaps one of the most fascinating studies involved a study of traditional Korean women with the culturally acceptable disease classified as "Hwabyung." The name could be broken down to Hwa ("fire" and "anger") and Byung (illness). Hwabyung becomes a "fire illness" (Kang, 1981) or "anger syndrome" (Lee, 1967).

In Hwabyung the liver, gall bladder, lungs, spleen, kidneys, digestive system or heart can be affected. Individuals present differing problems. Keh-Ming Lin (1983) noted that patients suffering from Hwabyung had suppressed anger for a long time.

Traditional Koreans tend to present bodily complaints instead of psychological complaints. Hwabyung is an acceptable illness whereas psychological complaints are not. The disease is particularly experienced by traditional women, many of whom suffered immense psychological trauma, sadness, disappointment, unfulfilled expectations, long-term suppressed anger, grudges and losses of long duration. Emotions are not given voice over a period of years. When suppressed emotions reach a threshold beyond which they cannot be controlled, they are physically manifested in Hwabyung. Unfortunately many die from this "acceptable" illness.

Hundreds of pieces of research exist on the physical effects of imploded anger (anger-in) or exploded anger (anger-out). For those of you suffering from an anger-related illness, or for those of you that care about someone who is, check some of the research in the Works Cited section of this book. The healing process can be aided by recognizing the effects of unhealthy emotional expression. Reading about anger-related illnesses and beginning to visualize the effect on the body of unhealthy expressions of anger can make the destructive process more understandable. Becoming more aware of what the body is saying can serve as a catalyst for change.

WHAT TO DO ABOUT UNHEALTHY ANGER

Know What Your Body Is Telling You

Individuals who have anger-related illness are often disconnected from their bodies; that is, they are not aware of what their body is saying to them through various symptoms and reactions. Individuals who disconnect from their bodies frequently don't know when their blood pressure is rising, their pulse is racing or hydrochloric acid is dumping into their stomachs. Most have no idea even when they are getting angry; as a result they seethe for days, hold grudges, displace their anger inappropriately on their families, rage at drivers, have stomachaches and headaches, grind their teeth, smoke cigarettes, drink alcohol to excess, eat half of a chocolate cake in the space of a few hours, etc. All these actions are means to displace or postpone one's feelings.

Knowing your body means taking time to focus—taking a few minutes several times a day to allow your body to speak to you. *Biofeedback* has proven very useful to many individuals with anger-related illness. Biofeedback literally means "feedback from the body." People trained in biofeedback frequently use machines that can provide a visual or auditory signal regarding physiological reactions. An individual might learn to predict an oncoming migraine headache by the cold temperature of one's hands. Warming the hands may reduce the intensity of the headache. Another person might experience neck or skeletal pain whenever standing in front of a group of people. Biofeedback equipment gives immediate body feedback, which aids in understanding triggers and teaching preventive relaxation. Your doctor might be able to refer you to someone who practices biofeedback techniques.

Your physician might also suggest other useful ways to become more aware of what your body is saying. Speak honestly and directly to your physician about your concerns and your decision to become more aware of the effects that unhealthy anger is having on your body. Don't intentionally or unintentionally withhold information from your doctor. Make your doctor an ally in your healing process. Many physicians can teach progressive relaxation or can refer you to a good massage therapist. Regular massage from a highly trained individual can strengthen body awareness.

Knowing your body also means learning to be a good detective: "My lower back is beginning to hurt. I wonder what happened before it started hurting." Being a good detective means paying attention, which can be difficult when caught up in the details of day-to-day living. Keep a journal that is small enough to fit in a pocket or purse. Use the journal to record changes that you are aware of in your body during the day. Sometimes you won't be able to make the connection between body pain and triggers right away, but eventually you'll see a pattern begin to form.

Some people draw an outline of their body in their journal and use colored pencils to shade in areas where anger has settled during the day. For example, through the drawings in her journal, a woman was able to become aware of an important anger trigger. She discovered that she had shaded in red her lower back and stomach areas each time that she had contact with a particular friend. Her friend, she became aware, was very controlling and critical, frequently giving unsolicited advice. The woman had never acknowledged her anger at her friend's behavior, but had experienced pain in her stomach and lower back with every interaction. She was eventually able to establish clearer boundaries with her friend. The pain in her stomach and back stopped.

A man shaded the area around his heart, lungs, legs, arms, hands and jaw every time he had to wait. Even when he had plenty of time, waiting was a trigger for physiological reactions to anger. He remarked at one point that the shading on his drawing appeared as if he was about to explode. In fact, as a sufferer of coronary artery disease, he was exploding internally.

Becoming Aware of Triggers

As mentioned in the introduction, triggers can be any sights, sounds, smells, touch, tastes, facial expressions, words, dates, seasons, holidays, ages our children turn, behaviors, etc., that cause us to react. Many people are under-reactors (imploding anger or shutting down) or over-reactors (exploding anger or acting out). Triggers precede the imploding or exploding of anger. For instance, John became aggressive whenever he felt powerless or vulnerable. A trigger might be his daughter becoming ill or the tears of a loved one. It is extremely important for John to understand his triggers so that when they occur he can be prepared to take a different direction rather than rage or acting out.

An individual who becomes aware of anger triggers may also learn where the triggers originate. The individual may then work on them by deactivating the loaded areas of life. Marie overreacted when her children lied. She had little understanding that her rage response occurred whenever she felt out of control; an aggressive response can block the feeling of vulnerability. Lying wasn't a moral issue, it was a control issue. Marie was going through a messy divorce that she didn't want. Her life felt "out of control" and had for some time. Besides the triggers themselves and the usual responses to them, she still had to confront the feelings under the response.

With awareness we can choose to react differently. One way to act in a different fashion is to use humor or to take a more lighthearted approach to respond to one's triggers. Another different way to act is to reach out to another person when a trigger is activated, because reaching out moves the focus away from our own behavior. We'll now discuss both of these approaches.

A Little Humor Goes a Long Way in Health

Ted came into the office with a smile on his face, which was new for him. I began to see him when he was suffering with severe ulcerative colitis. He had talked about many things he was angry about, including his boss and fellow employees at work. I had suggested that he write the incidents, people or events that angered him on the bottom of his shoes and enjoy walking around on them all week. He had worked hard in therapy and his health attested to his effort. He crossed his legs and I could see the words written on his left shoe.

"It's a good thing I have size-twelve feet," he laughed. "I was really taking things much too seriously last week. Staying in my own shoes helped this week. When I was at work I would start to get negative, but then I'd think of my shoes and I'd just start laughing. What a way to get my anger out. It didn't hurt anyone including me. I think maybe I'll be ready to talk to my boss about my concerns next week. I'll talk to him with my feet flat on the floor."

Ted had imploded anger for most of his life. The degree of his internal rage manifested itself in ulcerative colitis. Slowly, he had worked through a great deal of grief and been able to begin expressing his anger safely. He also developed a wonderful, healing sense of humor. He needed to learn that it was safe to express his anger and at the same time stand back a bit and achieve balance. His ability to laugh helped him view things differently from a distance.

Some studies support the belief that learning to laugh can save our lives. Physician and author Norman Cousins (1979) personally found a connection between laughter, which he referred to as "inner jogging," and the healing process. Cousins suffered from a serious illness of the connective tissue. He realized that there was a relationship between serious illness and stress and concluded that if stress and anxiety could make you sick, then perhaps positive emotions could aid in healing. He checked out of the hospital and began a regime of vitamin C and laughter. He watched comedy after comedy from his hotel room bed. He found that laughter not only caused a decrease in what had become constant physical pain but also began to turn the tide of his illness.

A sense of humor can also help save important relationships. One of the most intense arguments that my late husband and I had was in a video store. We had both had a hectic week at work (both of us trauma specialists). We also had five children that were at the time in full-blown adolescence (need I say more?). Our children were elsewhere on this particular Friday night, so we decided to relax and spend the evening watching movies. When we entered the video store, we noticed a couple arguing over the selection of movies. We of course were far healthier than that and gave each other a knowing and rather righteous look that said, "Can you believe those two?" Anyway, our agreement was that each of us would select a video because we had different tastes in movies. I was busy looking when my husband appeared with two videos. I repeated our agreement. He explained that these were really fine movies and implied that I could stop my search. One thing led to another and he said, "I won't get any then, you pick them." I said I wouldn't get any either and we huffed out of the store.

I sat loudly silent in the car with my arms folded. He started muttering to himself in Italian (a bad sign, but I wasn't noticing because—after all—I was ignoring him). We stopped by the grocery store and argued about who was going to shop. Usually we shopped together. We both got a cart. We both bought groceries. We returned to the car, and by now we were seething. When we arrived home, we both busied ourselves by loudly putting our separate groceries away. At some point while completing this task, we noticed that we had bought the same things.

We then finally took the same advice that we sometimes gave our clients. We stopped and looked at ourselves from a distance. Our antics, of course, were absolutely hysterical. Soon our laughter filled the tense silence and our anger melted. We were later able to have a good discussion about what had happened in the video store and the triggers that had been set off within each of us.

AGAIN, CONNECTION IS A CORRECTION

In our out-of-balance world, literally millions of individuals suffer the effects of real or perceived isolation. Gavin Esler, in his book *The United States of Anger* (1997, p. 13), speaks to the issue of isolation: "By the 1990s millions of Americans complained that America was ceasing to be 'great' because Americans were no longer 'good.' The opinion polls showed that in each decade since the 1950s Americans have been less and less trusting of human nature, of each other, and of their government." Although I don't share the impression that most Americans are no longer "good," the impression is understandable in light of the sustained effect of the media, where "if it bleeds, it leads"—that is, because people appear most interested in reports of violence, such stories often begin newscasts.

Most people today are afraid to help someone who is stranded by the side of the road or to ask a neighbor for help. Many people don't even know their neighbors. A large number of parents understandably don't allow their children the same freedom that they enjoyed growing up. After all, the Halloween candy may contain razor blades or the neighbor may be an untreated child abuser. Today many parents are frightened to let their children sell school raffle tickets to the neighbors or even send their children to school. People that I have talked to throughout the world feel isolated and disconnected from their families and their communities.

Unfortunately this perceived or real isolation has impacted many parts of our lives, including our physical health. Countless studies have shown that poor social support not only increases frustration, anxiety and the resulting unhealthy anger that contributes to the development of chronic illness, but also weakens our ability to survive illness.

Our health improves when we connect with others, share frustrations and help one another. It doesn't only take a village to raise a child, it takes a village to support the health and well-being of the adults that are responsible for that child.

In *Reclaiming Your Life* (1995), psychotherapist, Jean Jensen, presents the analogy of driving a car on an icy road. Many people step on the brake when the car begins to skid. Of course that's the worst thing to do because you've lost control. When triggered, many individuals "step on the brake": They surrender choice and react instead. An important lesson to learn when triggered is to "turn into the skid," find another human being and talk about what is happening. Sometimes "turning into the skid" involves feeling the vulnerability, the powerlessness, the sadness. When you allow yourself to feel the feelings without necessarily reacting to them, you regain control and put yourself back in the driver's seat.

It seems we often revisit "the chicken or the egg?" concept: Frustration, stress, anxiety, and perceived or real isolation contribute to unhealthy anger, and unhealthy anger can destroy intimacy and connection to others.

Whether you are a person who isolates behind a wall of hostility or isolates behind a smile, the first step to a healthier body may be finding one person with whom you can build trust. This person may be your significant other, a family member, an elder, a neighbor, an old friend that you haven't connected with in a while, a physician, a counselor, a spiritual leader, a family member by choice rather than birth, a support group—anyone with whom you can begin to build real connection. Be sure to select someone who can tolerate your testing because initially you will test, particularly if trusting others has been an issue.

As you begin to share your frustrations (talking it out rather than taking it out on your body), be sure to take note of your ghosts. Ghosts hang around and give messages designed to keep you angry and withholding: "I'm too busy right now." "They're too busy right now." "They have enough problems without mine too." "I don't want to bother them." "What will they think of me and the way I'm feeling?" "They'll just talk to someone about me behind my back." "I can handle this myself." "How's talking going to help?" "Trust is overrated." You need to overcome those ghosts that want to destroy you. Making a connection with other people is difficult, but your life may depend on it.

"I'm Not Angry, but I'll Get You Back While I Smile"

"Happiness is not the absence of conflict but the ability to cope with it."

—AUTHOR UNKNOWN

Several months ago, Ellen took the advice of her closest friend Diane and consulted a physician about nutrition. Ellen is a diabetic whose disease was becoming out of control because she wasn't eating properly. Now, after a few months, Ellen is proud that she has been able to stick to a balanced diet that is low in sugar and fat. She is approaching a normal weight, and her blood sugar is stabilizing. As her birthday approached, Ellen felt better physically and emotionally. She had more energy than she'd had in years. Diane had been one of her biggest supporters. No one was more surprised than Ellen on her birthday when Diane showed up at her house toting a rich ice-cream cake complete with fudge sauce. Her beautifully wrapped present from Diane was a three-pound box of chocolates.

Later in the week, Ellen confronted Diane on the gifts: "You know how careful I've been about my eating. That's why I wanted you to celebrate my birthday with me, because you understood. I was hurt and confused when you brought that rich cake and gave me the chocolates."

"I tried to give you a little reward on your birthday, that's all," Diane sulked. "I try to be a caring and helpful friend, but nothing seems to please you. I think this diet is getting to you."

Ellen felt awful. How could she have been so ungrateful? Yet, hadn't there been a similar episode with Diane a few years ago when she had stopped smoking?

Diane, of course, brought her own emotional baggage to this situation. She felt powerless in her own battle against overeating. Diane resented that Ellen always "came out on top" and actually believed that Ellen harbored feelings of superiority because of it. Diane was angry but never expressed her anger openly. Her initial support followed by the excessive gifts of chocolate first left Ellen with feelings of anger and frustration. After confronting Diane, Ellen felt powerless and guilty. Not coincidentally, powerlessness, guilt, anger and frustration are emotions that Diane has trouble processing in a healthy manner.

Diane has a "passive-aggressive" personality. Individuals with a passive-aggressive style, as the name indicates, can be simultaneously aggressive and passive. They intend to do emotional harm; the harm, however, is exacted in such a way that the actions appear justifiable as an attempt to either be helpful to or caring about the other person in the relationship. Being in a relationship with a passive-aggressive is like hugging a big, soft down pillow that is full of thorns. A person has difficulty believing that the thorns are there. The pillow looks so soft. A person who deals with passive-aggressive personalities keeps seeking comfort from the softness of the pillow only to get pricked again and again. In psychology, the term for this type of behavior is a "double-bind," which occurs when a person is given conflicting cues about a particular situation. Diane's original support and subsequent gift of chocolates put Ellen in a double-bind.

Passive-aggressive individuals learn early in their life not to openly express resentment or anger. Often they learn that they have to be a "good girl" or "good boy." They begin to harbor resentment at constantly needing to be good and outwardly compliant in order to maintain acceptance and connection with those they depend upon for emotional and physical sustenance. They learn not to confront situations directly but rather to achieve some measure of control through manipulation and oppositional patterns of behavior. They learn to express their anger sideways.

Significant others, family members and work colleagues proceed through a range of emotions during the course of a relationship with a passive-aggressive personality. First come feelings of frustration, helplessness, inadequacy, and lack of control, followed by anger and often guilt. All these emotions are the very feelings that individuals with a passive-aggressive style struggle against experiencing especially anger. Isn't it convenient that passive-aggressives find others in their lives to experience these feelings for them?

▲ ▲ ▲ ▲

Jason was feeling extremely frustrated at work. He was beginning to think he was a failure. Jason hadn't experienced this frustration at other jobs, and it didn't make sense to him. His supervisor was such a nice person, which made Jason even more upset about his poor performance. Jason wasn't aware that his supervisor set unreachable expectations, could never quite describe what was expected and often omitted crucial pieces of information when assigning tasks. The supervisor regularly expressed his "disappointment," commenting that Jason's work was "less than he'd expected" but that he believed in him. He said he knew that Jason would eventually do better.

▲ ▲ ▲ ▲

One of the greatest challenges when dealing with a passive-aggressive person is the ability to avoid double-binds. Keeping distance from a double-bind and avoiding being placed in the middle of one are difficult tasks, especially when you are triggered by the feelings brought about by the actions (example: guilt or powerlessness) in a double-bind. When interacting with passive-aggressives, self-awareness of one's triggers is important. By knowing about your own triggers, you can learn to know what feelings result from them and learn as well to simply feel the feelings, yet not act upon them.

Acting out on your feelings and confronting passive-aggressive personalities when you have already become angry and frustrated plays directly into their script, you act out the anger that the passive-aggressive has difficulty expressing. Recognizing your own role in interactions with this type of personality, then, is the first necessary step to stopping your involvement in the passive-aggressive cycle. If you are already caught up in the back-and-forth cycle that characterizes a relationship with a passive-aggressive, your behavior will seem hostile rather than proactive, which will continue both parties' cycles of behavior.

Jason is frustrated at work because of the double-binds his supervisor presents. One double-bind involves giving Jason confused, incomplete directions and only part of the picture. Of course Jason does poorly on the assignments. His supervisor then rescues him, lowering Jason's self-esteem. The supervisor scripts this action out of his need to deny his injured self-worth, lack of self-confidence, anger and powerlessness. Through these actions, Jason is made to feel the supervisor's historical feelings of incompetence and powerlessness. This scenario is most likely repeating a pattern from the supervisor's childhood. In this new version, however, the supervisor plays the role of the "competent one" while Jason substitutes for the supervisor's old role.

One way that Jason can escape this situation is to act on his own behalf rather than acting in his supervisor's play. Jason would benefit from exploring his own triggers. Why can't Jason validate his feelings that something is wrong at the job? Is someone being "nice" a trigger for Jason? Many people actually cover for a supervisor, or for a fellow employee who is putting their own job or health in jeopardy, because they want to feel needed or are hungry for someone to be "nice." Other reasons for this behavior are to feel powerful or to protect others from the anger they fear. Perhaps, also, they are still learning how to avoid another's double-bind.

Specifically, Jason may ask his supervisor to write down at the beginning of a project the exact description of the assigned task as well as clear goals and expectations. Jason is then protected from feeling like he's not sure what is expected of him. With complete information documented beforehand, the supervisor might be more reluctant to change the rules in the middle of the project. If valuable pieces of information are missing, the error will be apparent. Jason could also explain to his supervisor, "This job is very important to me and I want to do the very best work I can. Because of the way I want to work, it is important that your description and expectations are written so that I might give them my full attention." His supervisor may not stop using his passive-aggressive style, but he probably will stop using it with Jason.

▲ ▲ ▲ ▲

Ross is usually "Mr. Nice Guy," cooperative and supportive. Then suddenly Linda needs him and he's not there. As one example, he just had to go on a hunting trip when their baby was due. When I first saw Ross, he had recently separated from Linda, his third wife.

Linda came to the first session stating that she loved Ross but had "doubts" about his willingness to change. She had obviously felt frustration for some time because she immediately began a litany of complaints: "He says he's going to do things around the house, then never does them. The sink has been leaking for six months. He lectures me about wanting to spend money on a plumber but when I remind him, he says I'm nagging. . . . He says he wants me to take the lead sexually at times and also wants me to let him know what pleases me sexually. When I initiate sex, he says I'm controlling. When I let him know what I like, he says I'm shaming him with my 'directions.' . . . He never tells me when he's angry, but makes sarcastic comments about me when others are around. . . . He winds our little boy up before he goes to bed, then gets angry at him because he doesn't feel like sleeping. Who would if they've just been wrestled with and thrown in the air for an hour? . . . We drive to work together in the morning. He usually gets up late and then I'm late for work."

"Why don't you leave without him and let him get to work on his own?" I asked.

"I couldn't do that. I couldn't just leave him like that."

Ross sat quietly listening to Linda's complaints with his head down. When asked how he felt, he replied, "Linda's right. I could be a much better husband. But I do try. I'm not angry at her when we're with friends; I'm just kidding around. She used to like my teasing. She accepts teasing from everyone but me, I guess. I love my kids. I thought you enjoyed watching me play with the kids, Linda. I guess I'll just have to try harder to be what you want."

Now Linda had her head down. When asked what she was feeling she replied, "Guilty. First I'm angry, then guilty. He says all the right things. Then I feel like an ungrateful nag. It's like I've misunderstood him or been impatient and lashed out at him unjustly. I feel crazy. I'm in a double-bind. If I don't say anything, I get more and more frustrated. If I do say something, I feel guilty."

Guilt wasn't new to Linda. She grew up taking care of everyone in her family. Her mother was ill and her dad left when she was four. Like many children whose parents divorce early, Linda believed that if she had been a better child her father wouldn't have left. She felt that she hadn't taken good enough care of her mother. Linda felt guilty at the anger she sometimes harbored towards her mother. She had been her mother's primary caretaker, but at times she naturally just wanted to play like other children. Her mother died when Linda was a young teenager. Linda thought she hadn't been a good enough parent to her younger brother, who was frequently in trouble. She was still bailing him out of difficulties, trying to make up for the loss of their mother and absent father. When Linda felt angry, she immediately felt guilty. She wasn't passive-aggressive, she was depressed.

Ross knew all about double-binds. He felt that he had never quite measured up to his parents' expectations. "I never did things good enough. I remember in fourth grade I had to make a project for the science fair. I decided that I wanted to make a model of the solar system out of papier maché. Of course I left the project till the last minute. My solar system wasn't perfect, but I thought it looked okay. My folks didn't. Soon they were redoing it. They complained about always having to get involved in my school work. The model they built was perfect, complete with an electric motor that made the planets revolve around the sun. At the fair, they demonstrated the model while I stood back and watched feeling bad. I won first prize."

I asked Ross if he had felt angry that his parents had interfered in his project. "How could I be angry at them? I was a screwup even then, and they bailed me out all the time, just like Linda does now."

Ross had learned to assert his independence through resistance, procrastination, forgetfulness, obstruction and stubbornness. Just as when he was young, his nondoing mobilized others into action. By allowing Linda to take charge, Ross set himself up to be angry and rebellious. He felt worse about himself and angry at being controlled. He had learned not to express his anger directly, which continued his passive-aggressive behavior. As a child, this behavior had been Ross's opportunity for rebellion and pseudo-control as well as an outlet for the anger he feared expressing directly.

Ross was like a reverse puppet. When someone said "Lift your left arm," he'd lift his right or wouldn't move his arm at all. It was like some part of Ross said to himself, "You can't make me. I'm in control here." The price one pays for being a reverse puppet is choice. Somewhere inside, the oppositional behavior feels like control and a type of independence, when in fact all the puppet's strings are still intact. It is interesting that passive-aggressives fear conflict and avoid it at all costs, and yet they create conflict continually.

Part of the difficulty was that Ross was stuck in the bind of being overly dependent, yet angry at those upon whom he depended. To handle stress and feelings of inadequacy, Ross used the pattern of behavior that he had learned in childhood. The pattern is common among passive-aggressives, as indicated in the diagram on the following page:

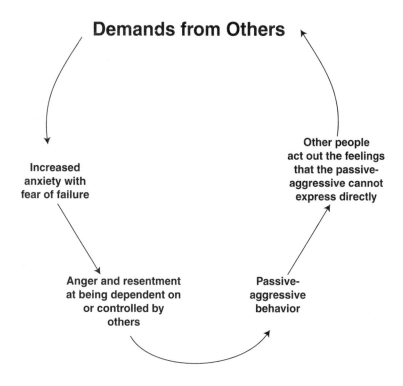

First, when Linda makes requests, it feels to Ross like demands. ("'Do this! Do that!' I'm tired of everybody running my life.")

Second, the perceived demands increase his anxiety and fear of failure. ("I've been a screwup all my life. This won't be any different. She'll just tell me I did it wrong.")

Third, the feeling of failure triggers Ross's anger and resentment at being dependent and controlled by others. ("If you think you're going to control me, you have another thing coming! You're not in charge of me! We'll see who's in charge.")

Fourth, his passive-aggressive behavior serves to allow him to feel pseudo-control and to release his anger sideways. ("Let's just see if you can get out of this bind. You're not so smart now, are you, because I'm in control.")

Fifth, Linda acts out his feelings of helplessness and frustration as well as his anger and resentment at feeling dependent and controlled. ("What can I do? I can't call a plumber and he won't fix it. I'm trapped. I've always been trapped.")

Sixth, Linda's requests increase, beginning the cycle again.

The double-bind in dealing with passive-aggressive behavior is that fulfilling demands (such as waiting for Ross and taking him to work) increases the self-loathing of the passive-aggressive, which increases the behavior. Rejecting the person will do the same. While in the middle of frustration, separating the behavior from the individual is difficult but necessary if the cycle is to be broken. ("I care about you getting to work, Ross, however, waiting for you is making me late. I will have to leave on time.")

FOR THOSE RELATING TO
PASSIVE-AGGRESSIVES

With the exception of solitaire, almost all games have two or more players. It is important when dealing with the passive-aggressive person in your life to first examine your own anger triggers. Quite possibly you are being triggered without your awareness. The result may be escalating psychological warfare.

Linda, for example, told me that Ross left her no other choice than to respond to his manipulation. She felt her only options were to respond to the manipulation or to leave the marriage, and the latter was hard for her because she loved Ross. Decisions are rarely this black and white, yet I could understand her feelings. People in relationships with passive-aggressive individuals usually feel cornered—in a double-bind. The important awareness, however, is the extent to which your own triggers are keeping you in the corner.

Linda, for example, had been a caretaker her entire life. Ross's "helplessness" triggered her caretaking. She couldn't let Ross find his own way to work when he overslept because she "couldn't just leave him." Despite the fact that Ross was a grown man, she spent more time trying to get him up in the morning than she did their five-year-old child, and with fewer results. Yet, the thought of leaving him triggered abandonment, which then triggered her caretaking. The difficulty is that under Linda's need to take care of others is a great deal of anger. Her anger sets off guilt, another caretaking trigger, thus leading to an endless cycle. Linda's caretaking served as a double trigger in the marriage. When Linda tried to take care of Ross, it triggered both his anger and his need to be in control.

Here are some important questions to ask yourself if you are in a relationship with an individual who presents a passive-aggressive style: Does your once-equal partner now feel like your child? Throughout the history of the relationship, have you become more responsible while your partner has become less so? Do you feel responsible for the behavior of a work associate? Do you sometimes feel double-binded by friends? Do you find yourself apologizing frequently for misinterpreting the behavior or motives of your partner, friend or work associate? Can you identify your role in the passive-aggressive cycle?

Passive-aggressives exercise their unhealthy behavior more effectively with individuals who have the following emotional histories:

- A long history of caretaking.
- Difficulty asking for needs or setting limits.
- Difficulty expressing normal anger for fear of hurting someone.
- Never feeling quite "good enough" and as a result allowing themselves to be victimized by others.
- Harboring a fear of dependency and therefore a drive to be in control of themselves and their environment (imagine carrying a hundred-pound box all by yourself even if others have offered to help you).

To help extract yourself from the grip of passive-aggressive behavior, you need to become aware of your triggers and responses, as we discussed in chapter 1. When you feel yourself being triggered, don't react. Find a friend and talk. Allow yourself the space and time to see things more clearly from a distance.

Recognizing Passive-Aggressive Behavior

Another way to avoid being placed in a double-bind situation is to recognize the common behavior patterns of passive-aggressives. The following are some common double-binds and some methods of escape:

Being Late

Regarding Ross's pattern of oversleeping, Linda needs to let Ross know that his behavior has become difficult for her. She could explain in a kind way that she cares a great deal about their relationship and doesn't want her frustration with his oversleeping to create space between them. She could let Ross know that out of respect for both of them, she will no longer be taking the responsibility of waking him up in the morning. She might explain that she needs to focus on her own responsibility to arrive at work on time. She will leave for work at 8 A.M. to allow herself plenty of time. If he is not ready, he will need to find another way to get to work—perhaps call a friend, take the bus, take the other car, etc.

Many individuals have told me that the double-binds presented by a passive-aggressive partner began long before they married or committed to the relationship. For instance, your partner promises to call at seven and doesn't call until ten. You "wait by the phone," growing more agitated. By ten you are furious. Instead of "waiting by the phone," you have the choice to continue with your life rather than holding yourself hostage. You can clearly let the other know of your disappointment the next time you are together. If you haven't been held hostage, you won't be full of hostility when you communicate your feelings.

When you begin making choices on your own behalf, your partner may experience anger. You have stopped the cycle by refusing to take on the feelings that the other person wants you, instead of them, to experience. Once you have dealt with your own triggers, true communication is possible. Covering your own feelings while assuming the feelings of the passive-aggressive is not respectful of yourself or the other person.

Broken Promises

Another common double bind is when a passive-aggressive fails to follow through on a promise. Your reaction might start out as reminding, but then it perhaps escalates to nagging and frustration, and finally anger. As the escalation increases, you are again in the position of experiencing someone else's feelings.

Ross promised to fix the leaking pipe and didn't. He also let Linda know that he would be unhappy if she called a plumber. If she chooses to accept these conditions, she is once again caught in a double-bind. A healthier approach for Linda would be to let Ross know the amount of time she is willing to endure the leak. After that set amount of time, she will take one of two courses of action: She will ask a handy friend or family member to fix the pipe (if she doesn't know how to fix it herself), or she will call a plumber. Once a decision about action has been made, the double-bind is released. Again, if this is done in anger or in a vindictive or hostile manner, you have already been triggered and you've taken another step in the psychological warfare.

Giving Unclear Messages

Jason's supervisor earlier in the chapter exemplified this aspect of passive-aggressive behavior. By failing to provide Jason with proper instructions about the expectations for his work performance, the supervisor could avoid his responsibility for any of Jason's shortcomings—that is, until Jason requested more specific guidance. When Jason, or someone in his position, refuses to become party to uncertainty or poor communication, that person breaks the cycle that enables the passive-aggressive style to flourish.

Picking Up After Oneself

One of the most common complaints that I hear from the significant others of passive-aggressives is, "She/he just won't pick up after herself/himself. I'm tired of doing all the work around the house. I pick up after myself. Why won't she/he do the same?" I'm not sure the desired response is to the "why" of it, but there could be two reasons: One, people simply have different styles of living. Some like tidiness, some are comfortable with disorder. It's not really a moral issue, but the complaint is frequently presented that way. Two, resisting picking up after oneself has become a tactic in psychological warfare.

My suggestion is usually quite simple. If tidiness is important to you but you don't wish to function as an indulging or nagging parent to your roommate or adult partner, simply put a box or basket in a location that is out of sight. If your partner doesn't pick things up and this behavior bothers you, put the offending objects in the basket for your partner to deal with at a later time. If this behavior has been a passive-aggressive double-bind, it will most likely stop after the individual grows tired of re-ironing clothes or realizes the behavior is not effectively controlling you. If the behavior isn't passive-aggressive but is simply a different living style, so be it.

Remember, the actions you take on your own behalf, or in service of a more balanced relationship, should not be punitive. If the solutions are sincere approaches to problem-solving and are communicated with respect for yourself and the other person, they will eventually lead to better communication. If they are threats delivered with anger, righteousness or hostility, the war will rage on.

Don't Personalize

When dealing with another's hurtful behavior, taking the behavior personally is common. Personalizing, however, sets an individual up for innumerable trigger responses.

Quite simply, don't take personally the behavior that appears to be directed toward you. Chances are this behavior style was well in place before the person met you. The behavior is simply the way an individual learned to respond to stress and anger. The behavior will occur with or without you. It is an ingrained pattern of interacting and a once-needed defense.

You will communicate and respond much more effectively if you realize that the behavior that appears to be directed at you is annoying but not personal. I often suggest that people put a large piece of paper on a desk or bureau at home with the words "It's Not Personal" written in giant letters. It's a good reminder and it will help you not to allow another's behavior to trigger you.

When responding to double-binds or hurtful behavior, state the facts clearly and acknowledge your feelings in a timely manner. Don't accumulate grievances. Try to be as immediate as possible. Confront the individual with your perception of his/her anger and invite discussion as to what the anger or frustration might be about. When a person with a passive-aggressive style learns that it may be safe to express frustrations and anger directly, a slow behavioral change often begins.

Let the individual know, clearly and without hostility, how their actions make you feel. One good way to begin is to let the other person know how important the relationship, job or friendship is to you and that's why communication is important. (Of course if the relationship, whatever its nature, has ceased to be important to you, don't lie about your feelings. Be sincere.) Don't accuse. State facts. If the individual becomes verbally shaming or abusive when confronted with your feelings, don't allow yourself to be abused. Explain that this discussion is very important to you and that it might be more productive later.

Counseling can also be an important part of healing, especially when exploring triggers and understanding behaviors, or if the relationship's dynamics include painful abuse. If you want to go to a counselor and your partner won't, go yourself. Some will say, "It's his/her problem, why should I go?" The problem affects both of you. If you want the support and the emotional awareness that counseling might provide, try not to let this "righteous ghost" enter your space. Attending counseling sessions doesn't mean you're "wrong"; it simply means that you are healthy enough to seek support.

A WORD TO PASSIVE-AGGRESSIVES: LEARN TO ENJOY ACTION

If you can recognize your own passive-aggressive style and are reading this chapter with a serious wish to change your own behavior, chances are that passive-aggressive behavior is no longer working for you. Perhaps you are having difficulty in a relationship that has become meaningful to you, you have been suspended from another job or your health is at risk. Remember that the choice to change is yours. If you feel controlled from the outside, change will be difficult because it will trigger passive-aggressive behavior.

If you have a passive-aggressive style of dealing with stress and anger, the style probably started for one of three reasons: One, you have felt controlled from the outside. The behavior at one time probably gave you the illusion of control when you needed to feel as if you had some personal power. As stated earlier in the chapter, however, people who act as reverse puppets are not in control. Resisting requests, procrastination and obstruction are not action but paralysis. Resisting may feel like choice and control but it is not: the strings are still intact. The next time you find yourself resisting, consider choice. Do you want to be late to work? Are the consequences worth it? Do you still want to give your power to someone outside yourself? Would you feel better about yourself if you exercised choice and action? Most of the time, the illusion of control isn't worth the cost of lower self-worth. As an adult, you deserve to cut the strings.

The second reason that individuals begin a passive-aggressive style of interacting is that they fear anger and its consequences. Ross learned that his anger would result in more isolation and abandonment. That may have been true as a child, but as an adult his nonexpression has become the problem. Most people learn a variety of myths about anger: 1) the release of anger is always destructive; 2) people will leave you if you allow yourself to express your anger; 3) anger is disconnecting; and 4) anger when released can't be controlled. These myths are just myths. None of the above statements refers to healthy anger.

Healthy anger is expressed in ways that are constructive, not destructive. Destructive anger comes from nonexpression, not expression. Look at your own life. You may never have physically "hit" anyone, yet probably your "sideways anger" has hurt.

Unfortunately, anger that causes separation and distance between people has probably happened in your life, or you wouldn't use a passive-aggressive style. You may have expressed your anger in a good way to individuals who had difficulty with feelings or a need to be in control. Perhaps as a result you were sent to your room, physically punished, abandoned, or made to feel that your anger actually caused someone to hurt (a parent became sick or said that you made them sick). It may take some risk to relearn the benefits of healthy anger expression. You can't learn just from hearing or reading about it, though; you'll have to experience the advantages for yourself. Although expression seems frightening and it may take some effort to feel anger again, one of the greatest benefits is emotional closeness. An added benefit will be that you will regain other feelings like joy and love as well.

The myth that all anger causes disconnection is also untrue. Unhealthy anger causes disconnection. The productive expression of anger, letting people know what's bothering you in a kind and assertive way, actually increases connection and communication. And, as we're learning in this book, connection can be a key to emotional health.

"I'm Not Angry, but I Whine and Complain and Yes, Indeed, I Blame"

"Fundamentally the marksman aims at himself."
—EUGEN HERRIGEL
ZEN IN THE ART OF ARCHERY

A number of years ago, I was giving a presentation at a conference. I was standing in the reception area talking to the conference coordinator when an individual interrupted our conversation: "I can't believe that in this day and age a conference corporation of your stature would actually serve cookies during a break. Aren't you aware that there are people attending this conference who may have eating disorders?"

I was amazed by the comment. I had just complimented the coordinator on the broad selection of snacks served at the break. There was fresh fruit, yogurt, cheese and crackers, cookies, vegetable platters, caffeinated and decaffeinated coffee and tea, fruit juices, and an assortment of sodas. I was impressed as there seemed to be something for everyone. The individual who interrupted us, however, obviously didn't share my enthusiasm.

The conference coordinator took the complaint in stride, explaining that she did understand that a number of people had food allergies, eating disorders or diabetes, and for that reason the conference provided an assortment of snacks.

"You obviously don't understand at all," the individual replied, apparently even more incensed. "If you put cookies out I will eat them. I don't want to. I obviously won't be able to attend the remainder of the conference unless I can make you understand my needs."

I was almost speechless, which is unusual for me. The conference coordinator continued interacting in a pleasant manner as the individual walked off, clearly still dissatisfied. "Does this happen often?" I asked.

"I'm afraid it does. There are those people who thank us over and over again for being attentive to their needs, but some people complain about everything. You wouldn't believe the things we're accused of and held responsible for. It's amazing."

Since that time I have become increasingly aware of the methods individuals use to process their frustration and anger at situations over which they feel powerless. The conference attendee in this case has made the first step toward emotional health by acknowledging powerlessness over an eating disorder, but believes that uninvolved third parties should be responsible for not presenting situations where that powerlessness might be tested. The attendee's method of handling the dilemma was to whine, complain and blame rather than accept accountability for oneself. Whining, complaining and blaming are frequently unhealthy responses to powerlessness that we'll discuss in this chapter. When whining, complaining and blaming, people only aggravate the problems they face. As we'll see, a healthier alternative is for whiners, complainers and blamers to take a more proactive approach and become part of a solution.

WHINING

Whining can be viewed as the sound of anger and frustration being forced through a small tube. For very young frustrated children, whining is a normal style of communication. On the developmental timeline, the whine emerges between an infant's cry and the more mature verbal request of older children. If, however, whining from an older child proves to be an effective means of achieving desired results, the sound can continue into adulthood. At that point, the act of whining becomes a dance. People who give in to whining assume some responsibility for its continuation.

Sarah told me that throughout her growing-up years she learned that if she whined enough she'd win. "Sometimes I'd have to keep it up for a few days. I'd always get what I wanted or be allowed to do what I was begging to do, but I never in fact felt good about it." Whining sounded like fingernails on a chalkboard to Sarah's parents, and they would eventually do whatever was necessary to make it stop.

Sarah's whining did not work well with her partner or her friends. When faced with their rejection and negative feedback, she had to make changes in her style of behavior. With many people, change only comes when a way of living is no longer working, or is leading to more emotional distress than satisfaction. In Sarah's case, she had to learn how to state her needs and wishes clearly and directly. She began finding solutions to problems rather than staying stuck on the "unfairness of it all," and she learned healthier ways to express frustration and anger. "I never really knew how powerless and angry I felt. I complained and whined constantly. I think I wanted some closeness in my life and that was the only way I knew to get people to listen. As an adult it didn't work like that. I drove others away. Looking back, I realize that when I was young I don't think I wanted things, although I sure whined for them. It was love, attention and a sense of personal power that I craved. I was also afraid of responsibility. I didn't think I could do things for myself or be responsible for my responses to situations. It was like I was always screaming, 'Please listen to me!', but my voice sounded like I was screaming through a straw. It's no wonder my friends stopped calling."

COMPLAINING

We all know individuals like the conference attendee to whom life always seems "unfair." To blame the conference coordinator for making her eat cookies when many other food choices were available is an unhealthy emotional response to powerlessness. Yet many people react to life this way. Basically, such individuals feel that they are powerless over their reactions to the events in their lives and that other people are accountable for their difficulties and unhappiness. People who are chronic complainers are often out of touch with how much anger they carry on a daily basis.

Sometimes people play a game we might call "Now I've Got You." You may have been involved in this game as either the complainer or the sounding board for the complaints. In the following example, imagine yourself as the recipient of the complainer's venting.

You are spending a much-needed quiet evening at home, listening to music and reading a good book. Your friend calls. He complains about work, how exhausted he is and that he just got another assignment from the boss. You hear him out, then suggest that he explain to his boss that he is already overworked. Your friend tells you why he can't talk to his boss. You then suggest that he delegate part of the workload to his staff. "I can't do that," he says. "These are really important assignments." He continues to complain and you continue to suggest possible solutions. Nothing that you suggest seems feasible for him.

As the discussion continues, your friend becomes calmer while you become frustrated and angry. What happened? How did you get left holding the bag? You worked increasingly harder to find solutions to his problems. He explained why each wasn't workable. The frustration, anger and powerlessness that he experiences on a daily basis are transferred to you.

One way to opt out of this game is to not play into the feelings

of powerlessness presented by the complainer. Do not ignore
your friend; rather you can simply offer empathy for the situation
rather than providing solutions, because perhaps solutions are
not even what's being sought. Even if your friend continually
complains about the same problem, you do not have to escalate
your own frustration and anger by becoming part of the problem
with him.

BLAMING AND THE BLAME GAME

The complainer in the previous section has found himself in an
uncomfortable position that almost certainly is to some degree of
his own making. By trying to do everything himself or by not
approaching his boss to establish a reasonable workload, the complainer owns some of the responsibility for his dilemma. His
usual response is to complain and blame his boss for his problem.

In the United States, blaming seems to have become a national
pastime. The rich blame the poor; the poor blame the rich; the
middle class blames everybody; political parties blame each other;
employers blame their staff; the staff blames the boss; the city is at
fault; the government is responsible, etc.

Whoever "they" are are responsible for everything that's wrong,
if you listen closely to the blamers' chorus. ("They" are never
credited with what goes right; mysteriously, that's where "I" comes
in.) One difficulty with blaming is that it doesn't seem to help.
One old saying goes that when you point a finger at someone,
three more are pointing back at you. The problem is that
more and more individuals today seem to have difficulty taking

responsibility for themselves and their own actions, choosing instead to play the "Blame Game." Let's look at three examples of the Blame Game in action.

On the ward of a hospital: *Mr. Jones has just survived a nearly fatal heart attack. "I knew the stress would kill me, Martha. Kids always yelling at each other, you demanding, the boss never satisfied. Look at me now. I almost died. I hope you're all happy." Mr. Jones is also a two-pack-a-day smoker, a heavy drinker and sixty pounds overweight.*

At a restaurant: *The vice president of sales has just given Richard a choice: to voluntarily leave an executive job he has held for thirty-five years or be fired. Richard is shocked. He continues to listen as his young boss downs his third lunchtime martini, "Look, Rich, you know I've always been in your corner. I know how rough it is so close to retirement, but you tied my hands when you kept confronting headquarters with their errors. You've been a problem, Rich. People have trouble getting along with you."*

Richard was stunned. "What people? Who are you talking about? My evaluations have always been outstanding."

"Ah, come on, Richard," the boss replied. "Don't put me on the spot. People talk. I'm not going to name names. Come on, make it easy on yourself. Just resign. I'll be in your corner. I'll get you a good severance package. Otherwise, I can't promise anything."

At home: *It's the last weekend of the month and once again time to pay the bills. The husband and wife begin their bill-time argument like clockwork, as their two children try to absorb themselves in TV to block out the increasingly loud and stressed voices coming from the kitchen: "If you made more money, we wouldn't be in this fix."*

"Oh yeah, it's my fault; right! If you'd stop spending all the

*money and granting those kids their every wish, we wouldn't be
spread so thin."*

*"I'm not the one who eats those expensive lunches. I'm also not
the one who bought Tommy those expensive skates."*

And on it goes. Not a solution to be found.

While blaming often appears to be a last-ditch effort at diverting onto another party responsibility for one's own behavior, the Blame Game can actually be an elaborately planned psychological ploy that has at its heart two deeper objectives: 1) to be better than your opponent at searching for enemies, excuses, and reasons for problems, behaviors, and anxieties; and 2) to rid the participants of years of shame and anger by placing blame on someone or something else as well as to abdicate personal responsibility and accountability. Although the game usually has at least two players, it can be played in isolation as well.

The Blame Game is quite portable and can be played anywhere. Basic strategies for the Blame Game include moves like "Because," "He/She/They Made Me," "I Can't Control Myself," "I Didn't Know," "Scapegoat," "I'm More Capable of Intimacy Than You Are," "You Don't Know How to Do It Right," and "I Care More."

Tools available for your use in the Blame Game are supplies that will help you stop your opponent from winning: "Gossip," "Chaos," "Putdowns," "Mudslinging" and "Sabotage." Gender, Age and Race cards can be played when needed. For advanced players, three additional tools can be purchased for the right price: Lawyer, Doctor and Psychologist. When you have these tools in your corner, you can compete for big stakes as you try to prove that other people, situations or circumstances are responsible for your injuries or behaviors.

The Blame Game found its way into national news headlines some years ago in a case that came to be known as "The Twinkie Defense." An individual said that he had killed two people in part due to his consumption of junk food just before the time of the killings. His defense was that these foods had contributed to his mental incapacitation. The defense was successful and charges were reduced. In preparing his defense, he went to the big-money tools of Lawyer, Doctor and Psychologist. Depending on your game plan, these tools can be drawn upon at your discretion.

The general rules of the Blame Game are quite simple:

1. Always be prepared to defend yourself in any situation with the firm belief that proving yourself right is the key to improved self-worth. To make a mistake is to be a

mistake. Shift the blame to someone or something else as quickly as possible in order not to lose self-worth. Always make someone or something else responsible for your behaviors, attitudes, situations, anxieties and emotions.

2. When cornered or asked to be accountable, attack or excuse in order not to lose face and power.

3. Try never to focus on a solution. Only focus on who's right or wrong. Remember, in the Blame Game, being wrong means losing self-esteem.

4. All players must agree that the situation is out of their control. Entities beyond themselves are responsible for situations, behaviors and reactions to feelings.

5. If playing in teams, always blame the members of the opposing team for your mistakes, limitations and behaviors.

6. See your opponents as potentially dangerous to your sense of well-being. A good strategy might be to view opponents as enemies or nonpersons.

7. Always look out for Number One. Hostility and aggression are acceptable in the Blame Game to justify your position. These ploys can either be expressed to your opponents or kept inside where they can grow and fester.

Going into the Blame Game, participants should know that winning means losing. By "winning," consider the items one loses: dignity, temper, self-control, sense of fairness, relationships, spirituality. A real "win" in the Blame Game would be a decision to not play. Individuals, families and communities all win when the

Blame Game is put aside in favor of accepting personal responsibility and consequences for one's own actions. Yet, as individuals feel less in control and less able to be accountable, they are more likely to play a game that makes losers of themselves and the people and relationships around them.

FOR PEOPLE WHO HAVE DIFFICULTIES WITH ADULTS WHO WHINE, COMPLAIN OR BLAME

We all know people whose favored method of communication and relating to others is whining, complaining or blaming. Sometimes the most important gift that you can give such a person is to offer them the truth in a compassionate way. Many people become so frustrated with chronic whiners, complainers and blamers that they end friendships or relationships without letting others know what they are feeling. The relationship ends abruptly: The whiner/complainer/blamer never knows why and is perhaps deprived of the opportunity to work toward changing the behavior that might contribute to changes in the relationship. Remember Sarah earlier in the chapter? Once she became aware of the effect her whining had on her partner and on other people with whom she wanted to relate to in an adult manner, she became able to recognize patterns and to begin to change her behavior.

Faced with the negative behaviors described in the Blame Game, you might benefit from knowing some positive guidelines that will help you avoid beginning the game at all. These guidelines also apply to dealing with whiners and complainers:

- As suggested in the last chapter, *Don't Personalize It!* Someone's complaining, blaming or whining isn't necessarily about you personally. The individual has probably been conditioned to use these three inappropriate methods of relating to communicate their wishes, frustrations and anger, as well as to protect themselves from a perceived loss of self-esteem.

- If someone who is whining, complaining or blaming interrupts you from something you are doing, say you'll set a time later to talk. Such people are frequently unaware of other people's needs.

- Set a limit on the time you are willing to listen to an individual complain, whine or blame. By continuing to listen, you reinforce the behavior.

- If you are becoming frustrated at hearing the same story many times, let the person know that you would be willing to help her or him sort out feelings and find solutions, if desired, as long as you don't have to listen to the same issues over and over again. You might also say that you are aware that she or he has obviously been bothered (by whatever it is) for a long while and that you want to know how you can be helpful, presuming the person is honestly seeking help and not just avoiding responsibility.

- If you find yourself playing "Now I've Got You" as described earlier in the chapter, stop! Don't assume the other person's feelings of learned helplessness. Listen, but avoid doing the person's emotional work for them.

- If you feel you are being blamed for another's behavior,

beliefs or feelings, don't take the bait, because you'll be starting a session of the Blame Game. Pointing fingers doesn't accomplish anything and usually results in hurt feelings for everyone concerned. Instead, state directly that you feel the other is blaming. Admit your own behavior. If you did something that offended or hurt the other, say so and make amends; if you feel that you did nothing wrong, don't own the other's responsibility. You might say that you are willing to work toward a solution but you are not willing to be blamed. If the blaming continues, suggest that you both take a break for a short time until you are able to explore the issues without blaming. Set a time later in the day or the next day when you are willing to continue the discussion. Don't allow too much time to pass as you can risk pushing feelings underground that will surely rise again when triggered. Communication becomes very difficult between people with unresolved feelings.

- Don't accept group blaming in silence. Group blaming is when an individual or group of individuals blames others and assumes by your presence your agreement with them. For instance, I was sitting with a group of people at a banquet a few years ago. A few individuals began blaming homosexuals for the AIDS epidemic and other societal ills. Many people at the table obviously did not share the same beliefs, but didn't say anything. I made a couple of attempts to correct distorted "facts" that were being asserted and let the blaming individuals know that I wasn't in agreement. The blaming continued. Eventually, I stated clearly that I didn't share their opinions and that I found some of their statements offensive. Soon others were able to share their opinions as well.

After dinner, one of the individuals who had been sitting at our table asked if she could speak to me. She became teary. She wanted to let me know that she was a lesbian and had been afraid to speak out. She thanked me for confronting the oppressive conversations at the table.

For People with Children Who Whine, Complain or Blame

First, remember that whining is appropriate for children who have not yet developed the ability to clearly express their needs and desires. For instance, a two-year-old doesn't yet possess advanced language skills or mastery of emotions. Whining can indicate that the child is hungry, tired, frustrated, hurt, angry, etc. Whining that occurs for these reasons will stop when you have found the solution to what is troubling the child. Parents and caregivers should try to keep in mind that at this developmental stage the child is just doing the job of being two years old and learning to identify and express needs and feelings.

If whining has continued beyond the appropriate developmental stage (the "age of reason," around four or five), the child has probably received a great deal of attention for the behavior. When a child whines, a parent's yelling or scolding reinforces the behavior.

Sometimes a child not sure of his or her place in the family directs energy into finding a place. The child might try to attract attention by engaging adults in power struggles. The key here is to ignore the behavior while listening to the child's needs. "I hear whining; can you say what you want or need in a different way?

It's hard for me to pay attention to what you are saying when you're whining."

Children are known for saying "It isn't fair!" when they don't get what they want immediately, when they are being disciplined, or when you won't allow them to do what a friend's parents allow their children to do. Again, the children aren't trying to make life difficult for you; they are just doing their job. They are busy learning from you and others in their environment the skills, values and limits they will require as adults.

In order to build healthy relationships as adults, children need a variety of lessons during their social development. Children must have compassionate limits set for them. They also need to learn how to delay gratification and that fairness doesn't always mean getting what you want. Children also need models who can show them how to express emotions appropriately, with tolerance and patience. As we discussed earlier in this book, modeling is one of the primary methods that children learn from, yet example-setting works in both positive and negative fashions. Children can learn from models how to blame as well as how to accept personal responsibility. Consider the following parent-child interaction:

David slumped in his chair as his parents confronted him on the note they received from the school. "According to the slip, you haven't turned in a paper this entire quarter in Mrs. Jones's class," his father stated.

"And you have failed almost every test," added his mother.

"What have you got to say for yourself?" his parents asked in unison.

"The teacher hates me!" David replied defensively. "She never calls on me and when I try to add my thoughts to class

discussions, she says everything I say is wrong. I've tried, really I have! She's singled me and my friends out because of the way we think and dress. She's got her own opinions and won't allow any others. You guys taught me to think for myself. Mrs. Jones doesn't like kids who have their own opinions. I'll never get anywhere with her. Please let me drop her class and transfer to Mr. Stevens. He's already my football coach and we get along great. I'll do great with Mr. Stevens. Please."

It was quiet for a time while David's parents thought over what he'd said. "I think your mom and I should support you. You probably will work better with Mr. Stevens. We'll let the school know you have permission to change classes."

David sighed with relief.

Consider the lessons that David's parents taught him to take into his adult years: If you don't like someone you're working for, you don't have to do your work; you can avoid responsibility and accountability by blaming someone else's behavior for your actions; if you have conflicts with an individual, the way to deal with the conflict is avoidance; and if you don't like someone for whom you are working, you can switch to someone else. David may also have learned that he isn't capable of doing the work. What was accepted from David as "trying" was not a serious attempt. Failing to turn in assignments was clearly not David's best effort.

If David's teacher truly was singling him out, that issue also holds valuable lessons for learning about differences and conflict resolution. His parents could acknowledge the possibility that he was being singled out while, at the same time, rejecting the blaming. They could help him come up with some useful approaches to the difficulties with the teacher in question.

Most healthy children at some point attempt to blame their behavior on something or someone else. The blaming might begin with brothers, sisters or imaginary friends, or excuses like "The dog ate my school papers," "No one else does," "I left my books at school," or "I hit him because he made me angry." In order for children to learn emotional mastery, responsibility and accountability, and to be able to experience feelings of competence, blaming can't be accepted as an excuse.

Some children feel so bad about getting away with irresponsible behavior that they actually exaggerate the behavior in order to seek punishment, or push themselves into a situation where they need finally to develop internal discipline in order to grow into healthy adults. Again, children take from the outside and bring to the inside self-esteem, self-discipline and beliefs about themselves. The discipline to be able to start and finish tasks is a valuable lesson and leads to positive self-esteem.

Some children also blame because they are afraid. Perhaps there has been physical abuse, or negative behavior may have been used to define who they are as people. These individuals need support in working through feelings of fear and anger. Many individuals who have not worked through the fear, anger and powerlessness of having been subjects of childhood abuse continue to victimize themselves and others during adulthood. These adults continue the Blame Game, holding their childhood abusers accountable for their current behavior. We were not responsible for the abuses of our childhood, but we are accountable for our behavior as adults.

FOR ADULTS WHO WHINE, COMPLAIN OR BLAME

As we've seen in this chapter, whining, complaining and blaming are patterns of behavior that usually started in childhood. Excuses were accepted and whining worked to the extent that you eventually were given what you thought you wanted. If you were like most children, however, what you really wanted was positive attention and self-respect. Instead of building self-esteem, acceptance of your inappropriate behavior only served to increase shame and feelings of unworthiness. For those who are able to acknowlege their tendency to whine, complain or blame, consider the following suggestions:

First, *understand that whining, complaining and blaming often have roots in anger and feelings of powerlessness.* Sort out your feelings under the behavior. Children are sometimes ignored or belittled for needing and taught that they must never make a mistake. Many individuals who tend to whine, complain or blame experience shame and low self-esteem, feel lonely and isolated, want support or are afraid of making mistakes.

More effective behavior for an adult is to *learn to state clearly what you want.* Perhaps you don't know what you want and will need some assistance from a trusted friend or from a therapist in order to identify wants and needs. Other people may know what they want yet perhaps because of feelings of unworthiness are afraid to ask directly.

If you feel like you're going to start complaining, whining or blaming, try *engaging in some physical activity.* Remove yourself from the situation to take a walk or ride a bike. Physical exercise can discharge frustration. Remember that your problem is not solved, but you may let go of enough negative energy to allow you to focus on positive solutions.

Ask for support and connection. Many people who complain are actually asking for emotional connection, and either don't know that's what they want or are afraid to ask directly. There is no shame in needing.

Learn to focus on solutions rather than staying stuck in the problem. This tactic for dealing with your behavior might entail taking some risks. For instance, you may not like what your boss is doing and you complain about her constantly to anyone who will listen. What you haven't done is confront the boss on her behavior. Risking is learning to walk with fear rather than avoiding it. If you have never confronted anyone directly, of course you are frightened. It is risky to change behavior, but it is also healthy when the change is for the better.

Try paying attention to your conversations with others. Have you talked about the same problem repeatedly without attempting to change it? Do you find yourself blaming others for your movement through life?

Taking action on your own behalf is a powerful step. Individuals who attempt to solve problems or rid themselves of anxieties and anger by whining, complaining or blaming tell me the behavior is circular. They whine and complain because of frustration, isolation and anger, yet feel more frustration and powerlessness after these responses. In other words, if the behavior isn't working, try something else. Repeating an action over and over again and expecting different results is like trying to find your way out of a forest while walking in a circle.

Chronic blamers tell me that the same circular pattern exists in their lives. They are terrified to make a mistake and confuse making a mistake with being a mistake. When confronted with having made an error in behavior or judgment, they blame someone or something else. If the excuse is accepted, they feel more powerless and worse about themselves than they would have if they had been held accountable.

One man said, "I have always blamed my behavior on someone or something else. When individuals accepted my excuses I felt relieved. But then came the feelings of guilt and incompetence. Then I felt angry that others didn't expect more of me or were afraid of my reactions. I felt worse about myself and a lack of trust in others, and finally the blame would start over again. The circle never seemed to end. I am now holding myself accountable for my actions. I feel far more powerful and competent and far less angry and guilty. I feel better about myself than I have in years."

"I'm Not Angry,
but I'm Depressed"

*"I have made a captive of myself and put me
into a dungeon, and now I cannot find the key
to let myself out."*

—NATHANIEL HAWTHORNE

I magine experiencing few positive thoughts or feelings for an extended length of time. Picture criticizing yourself endlessly, being confused about simple tasks like what clothes to wear, or feeling worthless, useless and plagued by guilt. What might it feel like to have little sexual interest, experience drastic changes in eating and sleeping habits, compulsively worry about your health, and endure a protracted period when even the smallest exertion tires you out? Imagine losing your sense of humor while food becomes tasteless, relationships with family and friends become meaningless, and conceivably even a slight annoyance causes you to feel tremendous hostility and rage. Perhaps during this period you actually entertain thoughts of ending your own life. For more than 15 million Americans who experience clinical depression every year, what you have just imagined is all too real.

The prevalence of depression in America is staggering. We seem to be seeing depression earlier and in greater numbers than ever before. In the United States a person commits suicide every twenty minutes. Depression has become a national epidemic.

Many different theories and opinions exist about the causes and the effective treatment of depression. As is often the case with research, there are respectable and valid studies to support many different outlooks. I personally believe that in looking at both causation and treatment, the wise approach to depression is to consider a combination of developmental, environmental and biological theories. The body has a head, a heart and a home, and sometimes we forget this fact when developing treatment plans for depressed individuals. In many cases in the United States, doctors are content to treat depression solely as a biochemical imbalance for which the prescription of antidepressants should provide an adequate cure.

The antidepressant medication Prozac has been available since 1988. More than 25 million prescriptions have been filled. In many cases the temporary use of medication can be an integral part of competent treatment. For a great many others, however, medication has become an attempt at a quick fix, encouraging a mentality where people feel that a biochemical change from outside oneself is all that's required, with no accompanying shift in behavior or self-appraisal. With such an approach, the problem still lies untouched under the surface.

The present approach to biotechnology and pharmacology reminds me of Aldous Huxley's classic, *Brave New World*. This science fiction novel is essentially about the effect of technological advancement on human beings. In the book, values and morality are forgotten and delayed gratification doesn't seem to exist. One scientific advancement in the brave new world is Soma: a small cubic centimeter of a drug that will clear "ten gloomy sentiments."

The response of the population to Soma in this new world bears frightening similarity to our culture's response to Prozac, "But I say, you do look glum. What you need is a gramme of Soma." (1939, p. 36) Rather than relying only on medication like Prozac or some other Soma-like substance, a more worthwhile approach to depression would be to address its underlying causes.* In this manner, a cure in an individual's life would

*In many cases, the temporary use of medication is a necessary part of effective treatment for depression. Please see the Appendix for a listing of these medications.

have a longer-lasting and more meaningful effect, and the individual could also feel some participation or involvement in resolving the depression.

Children and teenagers who are instructed to take antidepressants often tell me that medications don't really help. What they want is simply to have more adults willing to listen. S. Rado, the author of many early professional articles on the nature of melancholia, echoes this sentiment when describing depression as "a great despairing cry for love." (1928, p. 420) Love is not just an emotion that one feels toward or from other people. Love of self is just as crucial to a healthy outlook on life.

THE UNFAIR ODDS OF SELF-HATE

One of the symptoms of depression is self-hate. Self-hate is the inclination of people to blame themselves for everything that happens, to see oneself as deficient and deserving of constant self-criticism, self-abuse and self-castigation. If rain comes on a day when a picnic is planned, the depressed individual engages in self-ridicule for not planning the event on another day. "I should have known. What's wrong with me? Why am I so stupid?"

This inclination of people to self-blame is why Freud categorized depression as anger directed toward the self. In other words, anger that was not expressed would become internalized, causing depression. Depressed individuals frequently fear anger, equating it with loss of control, violence, insanity and evil. Anger, therefore, is repressed and denied.

Depressed individuals frequently believe they do not belong, are not lovable, are not good enough and in some cases should not exist. All self-hate is based in shame, the belief that "no matter what I do, I will never be good enough." People who practice self-hate subject themselves to an internal tyrant who rarely sleeps and who acts as judge, jury and executioner of the spirit. This inner oppressor judges aspects of the self as bad and in need of punishment if allowed to surface. The shameful parts of the person may include, but are not limited to, anger, vulnerability, fear or helplessness.

The Seedlings of Self-Hate

Self-esteem and feelings of self-worth begin to develop in infancy. The need to attach to a primary caretaker is a basic drive of many species, including humans. Infants begin to internalize beliefs about themselves by the way they are held, talked to, touched or ignored. Early on the infant feels like an extension of the parent and is sensitive and responsive to the parent's feelings, whether they are love and compassion or self-hate and anger.

This internalization process can be hurtful to a developing infant self if difficult life stresses or circumstances intervene and parents do not fully welcome the child or provide the child with affection, respect, kind limits and guidance. Perhaps one or both parents suffer from self-hate, depression, or alcohol or drug addiction. Perhaps there is domestic violence at home or the parents are in the middle of a messy divorce or separation. Perhaps another child in the family is physically ill, emotionally ill or mentally challenged, or perhaps a family member died and the illness or death has never been grieved. Sometimes a child's birth can also trigger the past traumas of one or both parents.

If contempt, rejection or disappointment is demonstrated on the outside, children—who generally are dependent, vulnerable and highly receptive—will bring those projected images inside. Through this process of mirroring and internalization, the child will learn to show contempt, rejection and disappointment for the shamed aspects of the self or, in some instances, for the entire self. For children, an image of a caretaking adult in their lives is crucial. The child's developing self is highly dependent on caretaking adults for physical and emotional growth, and rather than suffer abandonment some children learn to survive by joining the parents in self-rejection and contempt.

Children in stressful and shaming environments often experience repeated disappointments when they are deprived of displays of adult affection. Lack of adult bonding and attention exaggerates the emotional need for affection and attachment and prolongs dependency. Such children are vulnerable to disappointment and develop a derivative sense of self: "You're nobody till somebody loves you." Their self-esteem becomes dependent on external affection and approval. This need for external approval provides some explanation of why many young people attempt or commit suicide when they feel rejected by a girlfriend or boyfriend.

A fifteen-year-old boy described as a "normal, ordinary kid" recently ordered his girlfriend off the school bus at gunpoint, took her to his home and shot himself in the head in front of her. The behavior of this seemingly "ordinary kid" more than likely was triggered by rejection. He was in all probability full of rage, which quickly turned to self-hate. Suicide is an act of anger that is often accompanied by the hope that the person who finds the victim will be regretful and will suffer.

The Seedlings Grow

Individuals who grow up with self-hate also find themselves as adults who are deficient in self-soothing and self-caring skills, as well as being critical and judgmental of themselves. Their need for external love, support, comfort and affection is a double-edged sword. Because early needs for nurturing, affection and comfort were met with sarcasm, ridicule and shaming, self-hating individuals often despise even their most basic needs for support and affection. Many learn not to expect comfort from others but rather to expect blame, punishment or indifference. They have learned to hate their feelings of helplessness. Many self-haters promise themselves early in life that they will never allow themselves to be vulnerable again, so they may appear to others to be aloof, cold and immune to feelings.

Self-hate and emotional dependence feed on each other. Self-hate causes individuals to reject themselves and, as a result of self-rejection, to feel unable to depend upon themselves. They are forced into emotional dependence on other people and subsequently hate themselves for the dependency.

Individuals may also experience anger for the one on whom they are dependent. As stated by psychiatrist and author John Bowlby, "The child feels a longing for love that has never been met and, next, bitter resentment against those who, for whatever reason, have not given it to him/her." (1980, p. 239)

The individual becomes angry because needs for intimacy aren't met "despite all I've done." The person experiences anger and may even erupt. The eruption is quickly followed by guilt, then self-blame and self-hate. The individual works harder at pleasing people and repressing his or her own needs, and again

...ames dependent on someone else for acceptance. Self-hate follows a very painful and seemingly endless cycle.

LOSS, TRAUMA, ANGER AND DEPRESSION

Many life events can trigger depression: separation and divorce, death of a loved one, delayed grief, psychological or physical trauma, disruption in a life pattern, illness and loss of a job are some examples. The experience of loss and the accompanying feelings of sorrow and sadness are typical aspects of the human condition and should not be confused with depression. In normal grief—whether the loss is due to death, illness, loss, divorce or separation—the individual's reaction to the event is limited by time, manifests itself in proportion to its magnitude and follows a path to resolution. It's the incompletion or interruption of a grief or loss episode that more commonly leads to true depression.

I remember very little of the week when my husband died. Only now, while involved in preparation for a gathering for the year anniversary, am I asking myself basic questions like, "There were a lot of people who stayed at the house. I wonder where everyone slept." Neither my sons nor I remember many of the details of that first period surrounding Rudy's death. I remember not being able to eat or sleep for several days. I recall being sick to my stomach. I remember wandering around aimlessly for many days and crying so much that I felt there must not be many tears remaining. I repeatedly relived the last days of his life, wondering if there was anything more I could have said or done. I remember feeling angry at being left.

I was both angry and confused by the seemingly endless number of forms that I had to fill out and amazed by the coldness of bureaucrats. "Don't they know my best friend just died?" I remember thinking. "Couldn't they have at least said 'I'm sorry for your loss'?"

Gradually my energy increased and for periods of time the sorrow lessened. Then my sadness would be triggered again by a piece of music, a memory, an anniversary or a holiday. As time passed, the family had many discussions of happy times as well as many humorous memories of our life with Rudy.

As a child I learned from elders that it takes one full cycle of seasons to grieve a loss. I was fortunate during that cycle of seasons to have a large community of friends and relatives who upheld meaningful rituals and provided support and understanding to our family.

With many individuals who are prone to depression, this cycle of seasons during a grieving time is first denied them by their environment, and then later by themselves. When normal grief is unsupported and delayed, even a minor loss years later can trigger a downward spiral of depression. The response to this loss is more intense than the situation warrants and may be accompanied by pessimism, self-hate, changes in eating and sleeping patterns, loss of energy, confusion, guilt, loss of interest in family and friends, irritability and sometimes suicidal thoughts. Biochemical changes play a role in this downward spiral and will be discussed later in the chapter.

Environments characterized by persistent stress cause an

individual to become loss-sensitive. The individual might have
grown up in an atmosphere of stress or suffered the effects of war,
rape, domestic violence or other stressors. Consider the effects of
early stress on Joanne, a woman whom I counseled.

*Joanne remembers the day she "stopped feeling." "I was about
five years old. It must have been a Saturday or Sunday afternoon
because my parents were both home. They had had too much to
drink and were yelling at each other. My mother told me to get
out of the house. I went out and sat on the front stoop. I put my
hands over my ears and tried to block out the sounds. I cried and
felt like I couldn't breathe. I knew my mommy was going to get
hurt. She had been hurt many times. I didn't know what to do
and I felt helpless.*

*"My favorite aunt lived next door. I noticed that she was sit-
ting in her backyard with another adult. Couldn't they hear?
Why weren't they helping? I ran over to my aunt's house as fast
as I could, 'Auntie, Auntie, you have to help me. Daddy's going to
hurt Mommy. Listen, she's screaming. Please help! I can't go
inside. Please!'*

*"My aunt picked me up and put me on her lap. 'Now Jo, I
don't want to ever hear you talking like that again! Leave your
parents to their problems. If you tell people, the welfare is going
to take you away and none of us will see you again. Do you want
that?' I shook my head. I was terrified that I would be taken away.
I stopped crying."*

*Shortly after that incident, when Joanne was seven, her father
had a fatal stroke. "I remember being at the funeral, holding my
auntie's hand. I wasn't sad. I wasn't angry. I felt nothing. I
stopped feeling after Auntie's warning in the backyard two years
before. I didn't want to be taken away. I don't remember feeling*

anything after that," she said, tears streaming down her face. "I have been numb and depressed most of my life. I didn't ever tell anyone 'til now. I didn't want to be taken away. That day I think I lost any belief that there was help. I think I lost my innocence."

Joanne, like many people, shut off her emotions early in childhood. She didn't remember being angry, yet she suffered from a constant low-grade depression. She described it as a dark cloud following her around, much like Pig Pen in the "Peanuts" comic strip. She was amazed when her depression cleared. "I never remember feeling like this. I guess I didn't know what it was like to feel good."

Joanne's auntie loved her very much and, like most adults, never set out to hurt her niece with her words or behavior. She had been Joanne's support through adolescence and again when Joanne was depressed as a young adult. Auntie was in fact the person who brought Joanne to her first counseling session.

Joanne's aunt had also experienced bouts of depression and had come from a depression-prone environment. She too had grown up with domestic violence and had been physically abused as a young child. She, however, had told someone about the violence in her home and had been taken away by "the welfare" and placed in many foster homes. Her warning to Joanne wasn't from lack of love, but rather an effort—in the only way she knew how—to spare Joanne the pain that she had experienced. She hadn't worked through the issues of her own delayed grief, and she thought the only way to protect Joanne was to silence her.

Although Joanne had experienced a chronic low-grade depression for most of her life, she came into treatment during an acute depressive episode triggered originally by the break-up of a relationship and the subsequent move to a new apartment. The decision to end the relationship had been mutual, yet as Joanne was packing to leave, she felt forced out much the same way she had as a child.

As Joanne prepared for bed the first night in her new place, she heard the couple in the apartment next door arguing. She said she covered her head with her pillow but could not block out the sound of muffled voices. She said that she was wide awake all night, even though the argument had ceased shortly after she had gone to bed. "I lay very still, like I was afraid to move. I felt like I was five years old." Leaving her relationship and hearing the arguing neighbors in her new apartment complex triggered an acute depressive episode. It took several counseling sessions for Joanne to understand her triggers and to experience the anger and fear of the little five-year-old girl sitting on the porch. She was eventually able to feel the pain of the little girl at her father's funeral. She did what most people do when grief is delayed: She allowed herself to experience these other emotions when she felt safe herself.

Under Joanne's depression was a good deal of unresolved loss as well as cumulative trauma. Trauma occurs when emotions are stimulated and then the release of emotion is blocked. In Joanne's case, the domestic violence in the family stimulated both fear and anger. She didn't have a social support system to which she could release emotion, and she learned to survive by numbing it and repressing her feelings.

The importance of a support system in determining the course of depression is highlighted by Bruno Bettelheim's reference to concentration camp survivors during World War II:

"In the camps because of the depths of despair that often

pervaded every moment of existence, I experienced more keenly than ever before, and observed in other prisoners, how a small sign that others indeed cared—a message from home, a gesture from another prisoner, even an item in the newspaper which suggested sympathetic attention—could instantly rekindle the will to live." (1980, p. 65)

Delayed grief usually occurs for one of four primary reasons:

• Lack of social support.

• Shame of normal feelings like fear, sadness and anger.

• Unresolved difficulties and ambivalence in the relationship between self and the person that has left or died.

• Earlier unresolved grief and trauma.

Joanne's history upon the death of her father contained all four.

Veterans also learn to repress emotion; in fact, repressing fear is crucial to the role of a soldier. If a soldier's best friend is shot and killed next to him or her, how could the soldier stop fighting and seek the support necessary to grieve, let alone allow one full cycle of seasons for the grief process?

When a traumatic event occurs, the first feeling is usually fear. Fear will continue until individuals can control the trauma, or until they come face to face with their own vulnerability and helplessness. Fear will frequently be replaced by fleeting anger and then depression. One of the first symptoms of post-traumatic stress disorder is depression, and yet soldiers who acknowledged depression historically were considered "wimps," as was the case in World War I and World War II.

In the Vietnam era, many veterans were not supported because they were judged unworthy of support by people who labeled them "baby killers." As a culture, we blamed the victim. One severely depressed Vietnam veteran told me he was ashamed to ask for help after the reception he received returning from Southeast Asia: "I'll never forget the crowd of people booing us. Two people threw animal blood all over me and called me a 'baby killer.' First I was angry. Then I tried to rationalize and blame: 'I didn't kill any babies, others did. Go after them! I was a medic.' Then I hated myself for wearing the uniform. I wasn't home long before I realized that I was severely depressed. I couldn't ask for help. Remember I was a 'baby killer'; people like me didn't deserve help, and besides I could handle it myself. I started drinking and smoking pot pretty heavily. I eventually tried to kill myself."

Just as soldiers in war have difficulty grieving, so do many people in our society who are taught that emotions are not acceptable. Girls are still being taught that anger is not permissible; boys are instructed in macho, tough behavior, and their natural vulnerability is often condemned.

It is widely accepted that depression exists twice as frequently in women than in men, yet four times as many men as women complete suicide. Terrence Real, in his book *I Don't Want to Talk About It* (1997), believes these statistics may be skewed because depression in men is hidden behind symptoms such as alcoholism, drug abuse, workaholism, physical illness, bravado, and verbal and physical violence. He suggests that because depression is still considered a sign of weakness in men, as is an expression of vulnerability, men would be much more likely to hide their depression by increasing their hours at work, drinking to excess or being combative.

Citing studies that link depression to early isolation, Real indicates that "from the moment of birth, boys are spoken to less than girls, comforted less and nurtured less." (1997, p. 110)

Many studies indicate that one in four women will have a depressive disorder at some point in her life. Studies also indicate that depressed women have far greater levels of anger than women who are not depressed. Perhaps women's anger is hidden behind depression and men's depression is hidden behind hostility and combativeness. Men, for instance, are eight times more likely than women to exhibit road rage.

Many believe that women are far more likely to pursue counseling or medical assistance for depression than their male counterparts. I personally believe that only a fraction of men or women that are depressed seek professional assistance. Many of us of both genders also need to learn to ask for support and to accept the support that is offered. Others may need to learn to give support with kindness and compassion. We all could benefit from focusing energy on rebuilding communities that care.

LEARNED HELPLESSNESS

One theoretical explanation of depression that can have significant implications for today's out-of-balance world is "learned helplessness." A great deal of research suggests that an individual's perceived control over one's own experiences produces heightened self-esteem and guards against depression. The depressed individual, on the other hand, has learned a degree of helplessness and that any action taken on one's own behalf is futile. Depressed people often perceive that success is not determined by skills, actions, behavior, effort or performance.

For instance, consider a child who has been repeatedly abused. When the trauma first occurs, the child will feel intense fear. If the trauma continues, the fear will eventually be replaced by depression. Continuing trauma will result in a condition where the child believes that nothing can cause a change in the situation. Learned helplessness and depression seem to go hand in hand.

Many of us know children who are given what they want without working for it. They, too, develop a form of learned helplessness. These children are conditioned to understand that they will receive what they want regardless of their behavior, actions, abilities or effort.

Martin Seligman was one of the original proponents of the connection between learned helplessness and depression. Together with two other researchers, Seligman conducted experiments with dogs (1975). Half the dogs were restrained and given conditioning with tones followed by shocks.

Each of the dogs was then placed one at a time into a small box with a barrier in the middle. Each dog heard a tone that was then followed by a shock. The animals that had not received uncontrollable shocks prior to the test learned, after a brief period of confusion and anxiety, to quickly jump over the barrier at the onset of the tone signal, and therefore never felt the shock again.

The dogs that had previously been subjected to inescapable shocks showed a brief period of confusion and anxiety, demonstrated by running around the box for about thirty seconds. They then lay down and quietly whined, submitting to the shock. When the signal and shock resumed, the dogs repeated the pattern.

The same researchers and others have conducted experiments which show that when a subject has experienced repeated uncontrolled trauma, the motivation to escape decreases, and is replaced with anxiety and depression. Other research studies indicate that uncontrollable rewards also impair motivation and cause a state of learned helplessness that leads to depression. Summarizing such studies, Martin Seligman suggests that "to the degree that uncontrollable events occur, either traumatic or positive, depression will be predisposed and ego strength undermined. To the degree controllable events occur, a sense of mastery and resistance to depression will result." (1975, p. 99)

I frequently see learned helplessness and resulting depression and anxiety in children with learning-style differences. The child originally puts a great deal of effort into completing required tasks. When the child cannot learn the material in the way that it is being taught, he or she doesn't realize it is because of a learning-style difference and eventually gives up. When a child feels helpless repeatedly—no matter how much effort is expended—and experiences little mastery, the child will soon feel helpless in many arenas. Some children with learning-style differences are misdiagnosed with attention deficit disorder and placed on medication, which puts into the child's mind that problems can be solved with a pill (remember Soma?). Other children are simply being passed from grade to grade regardless of their accomplishments, which can also lead to learned helplessness because rewards are unrelated to actions. Many of these children experience bouts of depression during adolescent and adult years, stemming from the feeling that whatever they do, the results are out of their control.

Through my travels, I meet countless people who tell me they feel that their lives seem to be out of their control. I remember one man I encountered who was kicking a bank machine. When he saw me he became embarrassed and commented, "I know I just made a fool of myself, but you see it doesn't seem to matter what I do anymore. Computers are in control. Have you ever tried to talk to a computerized voice? What I do doesn't seem to make a difference."

Perhaps runaway technology (as in the case of the ATM), increased psychological trauma and a perceived chasm between governments and the people that are governed can, at least in part, account for symptoms such as road rage and sky rage. No doubt there are many more reasons for this brand of societal illness and perhaps even more symptoms of it. What is certain is that the link between anger, depression and learned helplessness—and the increase in all three—is becoming more obvious.

THE HEAD HAS A BODY

The last several years have seen a great advancement in knowledge about the connection between our emotions and our bodies. When we suffer from a severe illness, changes in our biochemical makeup affect our psychological makeup. The reverse is also true: Changes in our psychological state alter our biochemistry. In essence, psychological forces rooted in environmental stress and biochemistry are interconnected.

As stated in chapter 1, stress responses prepare the body for fight or flight. These stress responses are stimulated and mediated through our central and autonomic nervous systems as well as by substances that are released directly into our bloodstream. Stress responses essentially affect every body component, bringing about changes in heart rate, blood pressure, bowel function, digestion and breathing.

Many individuals who are exposed to trauma become terrified, then enraged. Adrenaline and a storm of neurotransmitters (*neuro:* chemicals that are produced in our nerve cells; *transmitters:* passing along information) known as norepinephrine, dopamine and serotonin encourage build up of fear and aggression. Without resolution, the cycle continues. As stated by physician Steven Hunt and nurse practitioner Regina Delmastro, "Thoughts, feelings and physical changes (stressors) evoke more thoughts, feelings and physical changes (stress responses). Subsequently we have the potential for a cyclical, self-perpetuating 'stress system.' In other words, fear begets fear, anger begets anger and tension begets tension. Physical responses and changes escalate." (1985, p. 24)

The stress response system essentially produces behaviors that will result in an activation-resolution cycle. If we do not resolve the stressful event, the system will remain activated therefore depleting essential neurotransmitters. Simply put, when one nerve wants to talk to another it sends messengers (neurotransmitters). Nerve cells use a method of communication similar to our phone system. Synapses are the spaces that exist between nerve cells. The neurotransmitters must cross the synapse in order for communication between cells to take place. After the neurotransmitter has successfully crossed the synapse and communication has taken place between nerve cells A and B, for instance, B releases it and sends it back to A. This process is called reuptake.

If this system breaks down in a particular area of the brain, an individual will become depressed.

Again, we have learned the prolonged exposure to an anxiety producing stimulus will result in the depletion of norepinephrine, dopamine and serotonin presumably due to the fact that utilization exceeds synthesis. There may be: 1) A depletion in the amount of neurotransmitters that are released; 2) an overstimulation of the uptake process (the cell may hold onto the neurotransmitters longer than it should) decreasing the amount available between cells; or, 3) the receptors in the nerve cells may refuse to accept the neurotransmitters. In essence, the imbalance or depletion of neurotransmitters leads to depression.

An imbalance of serotonin, norepinephrine and dopamine can occur because of psychological or physiological trauma, the triggering of unresolved trauma and grief, self-defeating thinking, or environmental stress.

Which comes first: emotional/environmental changes or biochemical changes? Who knows? More important is for the medical profession to understand psychological and environmental factors that lead to depression and for professional counselors to understand the biochemical nature of depression. In order to ensure competent and effective care, all three factors must be considered.

(For those of you that would like a more in-depth study of the biochemical aspects of depression, read John Medina's 1998 book, *Depression: How It Happens; How It's Healed.* The text is easy to read and understand and the illustrations are outstanding.)

Preventing and Healing Depression

Assessment

All of us have "bad moods" every now and then, days when nothing seems to go as it should. *Moods* don't last. The mood might lift after a good night's sleep, a walk in the park or a talk with a friend. In the case of depression, the "mood" doesn't easily lift and is so severe that eating and sleeping habits are affected. Dark days continue, filled with negative self-talk and feeling "not good enough." Sometimes thoughts of self-harm arise. Isolation becomes more frequent and enjoyable activities seem like too much trouble. This type of depression should not be confused with a "bad mood."

Depression also shouldn't be confused with normal grief. One woman was experiencing a normal grief process and thought that because she didn't feel good in a couple of days that she was clinically depressed. Both of her parents had died in the space of a few months. She was sad, wanted to stay at home, and felt vulnerable and exhausted, all of which are symptoms of normal grieving. If she was still continually isolating and was constantly exhausted after a year, she might be in delayed grief and experiencing a depressive episode.

If you believe you are already experiencing depression, you should contact for assessment a physician or therapist who understands the interconnection between environmental, psychological and biochemical factors.

The professional you see should be aware of and open to different methods of treatment. Then you can embark on a course

that best fits your particular circumstances. You may need prescribed medication in conjunction with individual counseling or
psychotherapy. You may profit from changes in body chemistry
that come with other methods, such as from aerobic exercise, natural remedies such as St. John's wort or light therapies (where different parts of your body are exposed to a variety of colors and
frequencies of light that are thought to induce biochemical
changes). If your depressive episode occurred after childbirth, you
might consult your doctor about particular methods of treatment
that are effective for postpartum depression.

Group therapy or another type of support group could be
beneficial. Perhaps increase your social network through volunteering for some type of community service, involving yourself in
a community sports team or joining an amateur theater group.
Some choose to work with a minister, rabbi, priest, healer, elder or
another type of spiritual mentor. The methods of healing
depression are plentiful, which makes it wise to work with a
knowledgeable professional who will help design the best plan for
you. You should be actively involved in choosing your own direction, so that you feel that you are in control over changes in your
body and mind. Answering the following questions would provide a first step in sorting out what type of healing action might
be necessary in your case:

- Have you seldom remembered feeling really good? Do you
  feel you may have experienced a constant low-grade depression for most of your life?

- Do you experience chronic recurring episodes of depression,
  episodes that may be severe and are frequently triggered by
  environmental stress, anniversaries, etc.?

- Is this your first episode of severe depression? Have you had a physical examination to check for illnesses such as thyroid problems or diabetes, which can also produce depression?

- Have you recently given birth? Have you lost your appetite or become unable to sleep? Do you experience feelings of hopelessness, aggressive or violent feelings toward the newborn, or perhaps even heard voices?

If you only experience depression at certain parts of the year, a significant unresolved loss or trauma may have occurred during that particular time of year and your depression is triggered by the anniversary. You may also be suffering from seasonal affective disorder (SAD), a malady in which some people are sensitive to particular seasons.

If your depression has been severe, you are afraid of injuring yourself or others, you feel that an untreated illness like diabetes or alcoholism is contributing to your depression, you are suffering from chronic pain, or you are mentally and physically exhausted, an inpatient program, complete physical exam, or a hospital might be your next step.

An additional type of depression that is beyond the scope of this chapter, but which a proper assessment will investigate, is manic depression. With this condition, you may experience episodes of severe depression alternating with manic symptoms such as feeling an excessive amount of energy, flitting from task to task, racing thoughts, etc. Manic-depressive illness as a rule responds very well to certain kinds of medication. It would be important to consult a counselor or physician.

A Word About Suicidal Thoughts

You should reach out for help immediately if you are having thoughts of hurting yourself or someone else. For a depressed person, going to someone else for help can be difficult, because isolation is one of the byproducts of depression. But thinking of physical harm is an indication that action needs to be taken.

We often alienate others or isolate ourselves when we most need a human connection. Reaching out to a competent professional is difficult, but communicating what you are feeling to another human being really helps. Actions that are necessary to healing depression are learning to trust, careful assessment, developing patience, working hard at building a supportive relationship, uncovering ghosts and realizing that the healing process takes time.

As much as the depression hurts today, you need to learn to trust that pain decreases with time, with support and competent professional help. If you seek help now, you may prevent the severe pain of another episode.

The following are some characteristics of suicidal thoughts and those who think them:

- Most individuals who have suicidal thoughts also have fantasies of particular individuals finding them dead and feeling sorry and guilty. The underlying dynamic is frequently rage and wanting to somehow get even. Sometimes individuals also have fantasies that they are going to be able to be an observer in the "getting even" process, which is delusional thinking.
- Individuals who consider suicide have usually looked at themselves with a cracked mirror most of their lives. They are

filled with shame and self-loathing. Before making the choice of ending life, suicidal people must try to have the opportunity to find a clear and honest mirror to give a true appraisal of their value, now and in the future, as worthwhile members of relationships, a community and society.

• When individuals entertain thoughts of killing themselves, they're often focusing only on unwanted parts of themselves that they wish to kill. The parts that are causing their pain are usually the tyrannical judge, jury and executioner that exist in their mind. Unfortunately, if these parts succeed, all parts die.

• Many people who consider killing themselves think they are making a choice. Unfortunately while they are having suicidal thoughts, they usually don't consider other options. By definition, this isn't exercising choice.

• Many are clinically depressed and have been for a long time. These individuals benefit enormously from medication for a period of time as well as counseling.

Imagine that it is a beautiful day and you want to take a drive. You get in the car and start down your street. At the end of the street is a fork in the road. You can see that one part of the fork leads to a valley with beautiful mountains on the far side. You can also see lakes at a distance and you can almost feel what it must be like to relax by those lakes. Unfortunately this road is temporarily under construction. A man with a backhoe is momentarily blocking the road, but you are assured that the stop sign will be removed shortly. The driving might be slow and rough for a short period, but the workers assure you that the difficult drive is worth it. Although the pain may be unbearable for a time, with hard work the pain will lessen and hope will return.

The second road is a dead end. Suicide is literally a "dead end." Which road would you choose?

FINDING AN HONEST MIRROR

As we discussed in the previous section, finding an honest mirror is crucial so that a suicidal person can benefit from a more objective assessment of one's situation than that provided by a depressed and perhaps a biochemically altered mind. An important childhood lesson that I learned from a wise elder is the value of an honest mirror. When looking in an honest mirror, individuals see the reflection of their true selves rather than the misshapen image they perceive is there.

Finding a medical, psychological or spiritual professional to be your honest mirror is usually not a simple task. Qualities to look for are honesty, genuineness, spontaneity, ability to confront, empathy and a good sense of humor. You will project lots of your own misperceptions, expectations, thoughts, beliefs and emotions on them. That's part of your job, and a significant part of the healing process. The therapist or counselor's job is to reflect the images back while keeping the mirror clear.

Harold Belmont occasionally works with me in conducting five-day trauma interventions in communities. Frequently, one or two individuals in each training session immediately fear Harold or feel a great deal of anger toward him. Not even a secure person like Harold enjoys being this kind of target. When he acknowledged discomfort in these situations, I told him that I thought he

had a gift and that I believed his discomfort came with the terri-
tory of being an honest mirror.

At the end of the five days, the individuals who once felt angry
or feared Harold frequently love him with the same intensity. A
few of these fearful and angry individuals have asked him to be
their adopted father. Harold hadn't changed over the five-day
period, but the participants had. Their mirrors were clearing, the
shame had lessened and they had begun the journey from self-
hate to self-esteem.

Exploring the Landscape

Depression tends to be a shame-based illness. We may have
learned that our anger was bad, it was bad to be vulnerable and
have needs, our tears were bad, our beliefs were bad, our sexual
feelings were dirty, we were stupid, and so on. Psychological
injuries not only create wounds but also put up defenses against
such wounds occurring again. The problem is that we frequently
are not familiar with our emotional landscape and that the
defenses we erect might be as harmful as they are helpful.

The following exercise has been valuable for the individuals
I've worked with in plotting out their own emotional landscapes.
The exercise was developed from the theories of an early psycho-
analyst, Alfred Adler, and later Adlerians such as Benard Shulman
(1973).

Exploring the Impact of Shame

Materials needed: Plain white sheets of paper, colored crayons, markers or colored pencils.

1. Draw an early memory of shame.

The shameful memory could have taken place at home, school, church, in the community, at a friend's house, etc. If you feel ashamed to draw a picture because it won't be good enough, it probably means you were either shamed in art class or constantly compared to a more artistic brother or sister.

2. When you are finished drawing your picture, think about the child in that picture and what that child felt and learned that day. Turn your paper over and answer the following questions for that child. (Think only of that one memory that day. That day I learned _____ .):

I am _____.

Life is _____.

People are _____.

Therefore, I will _____.

(Consider the perceptions of this fourteen-year-old suicidal youth:

I am *not good enough, an embarrassment to others.*

Life is *for others but not for me.*

People are *critical and abandoning.*

Therefore I will *stop trying and give up.*)

Do you still believe the perception of yourself, people and life that you formed from this one early memory of shame? Are you still practicing the "therefore, I will"? Chances are if you haven't changed your perception of yourself, you haven't changed your survival adaptation—that is, the way you have learned to move through life. A child who learned that he or she was bad, that life was hurtful or that people were judgmental might have survived by learning to be invisible, learning to run or learning to rebel. We all have millions of stored memories; they may be full of shame, pride, self-disgust, honor or a variety of other feelings. Through each experience, we learned more about ourselves, life and people. We also learned how to move through life. When we understand the beliefs we carry about ourselves and others, we can begin changing our negative self-talk. It's important to understand that the words we use on ourselves came from somewhere. We didn't make them up.

Chances are if you are depressed, you learned many perceptions that were not accurate. Before understanding the misperceptions we carry, we need to change them. As self-defeating thoughts and behaviors change, the tide of depression begins to turn, allowing individuals to embark on their own course.

MASTERY

A very old and wise proverb states: "If you give a man a fish, you feed him for a day. If you teach a man to fish, you feed him for a lifetime." In successful therapy, one of the therapist's major roles is to help individuals believe that they are worthwhile as well as the masters of their own destinies. The therapist is a teacher and a mirror.

As stated by Martin Seligman, "A sense of worth, mastery, or self-esteem cannot be bestowed. It can only be earned. If it is given away, it ceases to be worth having, and it ceases to contribute to individual dignity." (1975, p. 179)

Ask anyone who is depressed, "Does it make you feel better for me to tell you that you are a good person?" If it was that simple, we could conquer depression by compulsively reading affirmation books.

Many individuals suffering from depression have believed that they have been ineffectual for most of their lives, regardless of their nice home, professional accomplishments or the number of times their partner has told them that they are "really a good person." As they begin to make changes in therapy, the tendency of individuals prone to depression is to give the credit for change to the therapist, the medication, their partner, their children, their new boss . . . anyone but themselves.

People have done simple things that have made a difference in their feelings of competency: One woman's clothes dryer was broken and she couldn't afford to fix it. Instead of feeling helpless, she began hanging her clothes on a line outside.

One man, feeling alone in a new city, bought a dog and began to volunteer at a local homeless shelter on weekends. "This was the first Christmas that I haven't felt alone in a long while. It's good to have company and focus my attention on someone else for a change."

Another woman, who felt controlled as she waited faithfully and endlessly for a promised call from her significant other, began asking friends to the movies or to come over to play board games. "I didn't have to be out of control. I could get on with my life."

One man who hated the thought of taking antidepressants began a regime of aerobic exercise to attempt to change his body chemistry and feel more in control of his life. He also changed his diet and his habit of filling his life with work. "I was arguing with my doctor all the time about taking medications, but I wasn't doing anything proactive."

It's important to understand that as you begin to take control of your life, the tyrant inside might yell even louder, trying to defeat everything you want to do. One woman had been attempting to clean up a room in her house for years. She could never throw anything away. The tyrant kept right at her: "What are you doing? You may need that someday. Can't you do anything right?" She finally painted a life-sized portrait of her perception of the internal tyrant and sat it in a chair outside. She was finally able to complete the task.

"I'm Not Angry, but I Sure Will Talk Bad About You"

"Things will continue to get worse until enough of us wake up and take charge. . . . Power and responsibility are connected. If you choose not to take responsibility, you cannot have power."

—SHARIF M. ABDULLAH

I t had been a good year for Allen. He had worked hard and his efforts had paid off. The conference he had chaired had been extraordinarily successful. He had also been surprised by an award for accomplishments in his field. Yet Allen did not feel much like celebrating. It seemed that the price he had paid for his achievements was the loss of some good friends. He once thought they would have been celebrating his success with him.

Trustworthy individuals had been telling Allen for weeks that two of his closest friends—fellow Native Americans—had been spreading malicious gossip about him and had been attempting to ruin his reputation. They had also stopped talking to him and would become stiff and awkward in his presence. He had tried to speak with them to no avail. He couldn't figure out what he had done to encourage such aggressive behavior from those he had once considered good friends.

Allen's experience is common for individuals from oppressed groups all over the world who feel the painful effects of lateral violence.

"Lateral violence" is the shaming, humiliating, damaging, belittling and sometimes violent behavior directed toward a member of a group by other members of the same group: African-American against African-American, woman against woman, employee against employee, brother against brother, Native American against Native American, homosexual against homosexual, Irish against Irish, etc. Other terms for the same behavior include horizontal violence and autogenocide. Lateral violence is most often applied to the behaviors of oppressed groups.

When a powerful oppressor has directed oppression against a group for a period of time, members of the oppressed group feel powerless to fight back and they eventually turn their anger against each other. In her autobiography, Angela Davis talks about her childhood classmates fighting "the meanness of Birmingham while they sliced the air with knives and punched black faces because they couldn't reach white ones."

From the Highlands of Scotland to the First Nations People of Canada, from the developing Czech Republic to inner-city Los Angeles, lateral violence within communities prevents efforts to heal the effects of oppression. Religious wars and ethnic cleansing develop as people fight each other over issues of bloodism (rejection or acceptance because of the color of one's skin, or because one member of a race is darker or lighter than another, mixed bloods oppressed by full bloods, or the reverse) or personal belief. Besides bloodism, some of the other symptoms of lateral violence are gossip, put-downs, belittling, competition, religious wars, family feuds, physical violence and gang wars.

Illustration of Lateral Violence

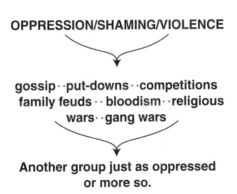

OPPRESSION/SHAMING/VIOLENCE

gossip··put-downs··competitions
family feuds··bloodism··religious
wars··gang wars

Another group just as oppressed
or more so.

An individual who is practicing lateral violence shows a lack of respect for, and denies the rights of, another individual. Oppressed people frequently take on the values, beliefs and tactics of the oppressor and begin waging war against one another. Many worthy goals and plans have been destroyed because of infighting, fault-finding, putdowns, gossip and scapegoating. When I am asked to consult with corporations, for instance, and find employee fighting employee, I frequently find oppressive managers.

Allen's story at the beginning of the chapter is a common one. Instead of celebrating one another's accomplishments, people in oppressed groups frequently feel competition and jealousy regarding each other's achievements. It's a bit like watching crabs that have been captured in a bucket. Eventually one of the imprisoned crabs will carefully climb to the top of the bucket, almost making it to freedom, until the other crabs pull it back down.

Individuals who suffer the painful effects of lateral violence commonly begin to develop increasingly lower self-worth, eventually believing that their actions have caused the aggressive behaviors directed against them. After seeing the reactions to his accomplishments, Allen repeatedly questioned, "What did I do?"

THE NATURE OF OPPRESSION

Oppression results when any group exploits another with the intention of hindering their freedom of expression, self-assertion or personal power. Behavior directed toward an individual or group is oppressive when it denies individuals their humanity. The oppressor fails to recognize the subjects of the oppression as people with dignity and rights, and they are transformed into objects not worthy of respect. Oppressors believe it is their right to make anything and everything an object of their purchasing power. In other words, the mentality of the oppressor is that "I own you and all you possess. I have the right to strip you of your beliefs, values and self-respect in the process of attaining my own goals. I have the right to destroy you if you refuse to cooperate in my procurement of power."

Even though oppressors share common traits, sometimes we are as guilty of stereotyping all oppressors as oppressors are of stereotyping their victims. Not all men, people of European descent, managers or religious leaders are oppressive. When people think in this manner, they deny the support of others in the battle against domination.

Just as oppressors don't all share the same traits, the methods of oppression vary also and are not limited to physical domination. Oppressors accomplish their objectives in many ways. The following list provides five examples of the many methods used to achieve domination. As you read about them, try to think of their application to lateral violence.

Creating Financial Dependence

Power is attained by making one group or individual financially dependent on another. Consider, for instance, the oppression of women by men. Historically women were considered the property of men and were rendered totally financially dependent. Although much has changed in this regard, a look at most magazines' year-end reviews of America's wealthiest show that a large proportion of the wealth in the United States today is still controlled by white men, who make up only a fraction of the population.

Although many people want to believe that the welfare system has been beneficial to American society, we are realizing that it has only increased the cycle of learned helplessness within oppressed groups. Millions are kept financially dependent for years at a time, some families for generations. One aspect of this learned helplessness is that people may receive monetary assistance without expectations. People who feel dependent experience a lack of personal power that is reinforced over time. A wise person once said, "Be wary of those bearing too many gifts. They may have gifts in one hand, but there are often chains in the other."

Eliminating Cultural Identity

In early American history, colonists and the prevailing white culture banned the traditional songs, dances, ceremonies, language and spirituality of Africans and Native Americans. They instead were forced to suppress and keep hidden their own beliefs or adopt the beliefs of their oppressors. Thus, important ceremonies for grieving, rites of passage and celebration—which had been in place for centuries, and in the case of Africans had been transported across an ocean—were forbidden. Additionally, when people are relocated from their land and denied their language, a great deal of the foundation of culture is destroyed.

For oppression to succeed, the oppressed must be convinced of their intrinsic inferiority. Psychologist Na'im Akbar speaks to the continued development of cultural self-hate and inferiority among African-Americans in his book *Chains and Images of Psychological Slavery* (1984, p. 49):

> *Black children sit at their dinner tables where a black daddy and a black mamma have often overcome racist opposition to provide them with food, and over the table hangs a picture to*

which they bow their heads, looking at twelve Caucasians sitting around their table at the last supper. There sits 'God's son' and all of his 'closest companions,' and not even the cook, the server, or the busboy is to look like them. The 'mother' Madonna is Caucasian, all of God's friends are portrayed as Caucasian.

Michelangelo went all out and portrayed God Himself with a long white beard to match his long white face, and the Heavenly Hosts were all portrayed in the same flesh.

Breaking Down the Family

One of the fastest ways to assure the cultural oppression of a group is to destroy family life and to take its children. Many indigenous populations of the world, for instance, had their children taken away as early as age four and placed in residential schools or boarding schools by mandate of the government. In these schools, the children were frequently brutally punished for speaking the language of their home or practicing their cultural beliefs. Because most schools were governed by one of many churches, the beliefs of that particular religious order were instilled. In some cases, brothers and sisters were sent to separate schools run by different religious orders, increasing the division between family members. In most cases, the children were denied access to their families for months on end. Many children did not have contact with family and community for years.

Countless children returned unable to speak their language and without knowledge of their traditions. They felt alienated from the family and community they had once depended upon for support. Because of forced institutionalization, most returned without parenting skills. The values, beliefs, discipline and skills they had to pass on to their own children were not those of their own people but those of the oppressor.

Many parents and other family members began abusing alcohol when their children were taken away. Many older people have told me that the women in their communities never even drank alcohol until their children were taken.

These residential schools or boarding schools for indigenous populations were not a part of ancient history. Native American and First Nations children were still being taken in the 1950s. Most adults of European heritage that I have spoken to, however, have never heard of the residential schools, and feel both anger and sadness when learning of the forced separation and institutionalization of indigenous children.

The separation of the family also occurred within the Jewish population during the Holocaust of the 1930s and 1940s in Europe. Children, elders, men and women were separated in the concentration camps; thousands were killed; many never saw extended family or lived with members of their original communities again. Some people have told me that, through their experiences in the ghettos and the camps, they learned not to trust many other Jewish people who they felt "sold them out."

Slavery tore apart the African family. Slaves had no rights and weren't allowed to marry. For the most part, families were not allowed.

As we discussed in the last chapter, children are by nature emotionally, physically and financially dependent on adults. When the parents in a family are physically, sexually or emotionally abusive, brothers and sisters also turn on each other, with comments such as, "If you'd only shut up they wouldn't drink." As adults, the children in these families often feel so emotionally separated from their siblings that they feel like orphans. Siblings fighting siblings in oppressive family systems present a classic example of lateral violence. This fighting between siblings is far more severe than normal sibling rivalry and extends into adulthood.

Undermining Leadership

In order to successfully oppress a group of people, one must establish distrust of leaders who might emerge within the group. Members of the oppressed group must distrust or fear identification with emerging leaders in order to ensure continued domination.

One technique for instilling fear is severely punishing "uppity" emerging leaders in front of other group members. In oppressive work situations, emerging leaders are fired. In oppressed cultures, people perceived as troublemakers were severely beaten and sometimes killed in front of their compatriots.

Another way to undermine leadership is for the oppressor to select individuals from within the group to be utilized against their own people: Many such "leaders" chosen by the oppressor are individuals who show leadership potential and may become a threat if not recruited. In order for individuals to be used against their own people, they must function on fear, or must hunger for the status, power and lifestyle of their oppressor. Most leaders recruited in this manner are unaware that they are being used.

Dividing and Conquering

Keeping the oppressed alienated from one another and deepening rifts between members of the group are effective oppression tactics. Greater alienation makes it easier to keep divisions in place. Communication between dominated individuals is a serious threat to oppression. Unity of oppressed people is to be avoided at all costs.

Divisions among a people are perpetuated by encouraging lateral violence and bloodism, funding wars, establishing internal oppressors and offering the illusion of power. I believe that lateral violence is the last step in oppression. If people continue undermining each other, fighting amongst themselves, and attempting to destroy each other's credibility and self-esteem, they are finishing the oppressors' work. They are imprisoning themselves. One government official recently commented on a community where a battle for leadership had ended in violence, "They can't blame us this time. They are killing each other."

How Does Lateral Violence Develop?

Lateral violence within oppressed groups develops in various ways and continues for a variety of reasons. First we will discuss the self-hate that is necessary for lateral violence to exist and then we will consider ways to stop it.

Identification with the Aggressor

When individuals feel inferior, inadequate and afraid, they take on the qualities of the oppressor as a way of acquiring strength and an illusion of power. Just as children internalize the image of themselves that the adults in their lives project, individuals who are oppressed internalize what the oppressor believes about them. The oppressed frequently assume the stereotypes that have been projected: We are inferior, untrustworthy, lazy, alcoholic, violent, manipulative, and so on. A young man whose family had immigrated from Puerto Rico told me the pain he experienced when his first instinct upon seeing his newborn daughter was to turn away. "I wanted her skin to be fair. Can you believe it? I was disgusted that my child's skin looked like mine."

Many individuals from oppressed groups immediately distrust anyone in a leadership position who is a member of their own gender, sexual orientation or race. These leaders may have been fully supported and considered "our only hope" the day before they were appointed or elected into a leadership position, but assuming the position causes many former supporters to change their minds.

I have been a member of hiring panels where a member of an oppressed group will vote not to hire or promote one of their own group members even though they are qualified and hold a flawless work history. Some reasons that have been given for their lack of support are "They can't be trusted working in their own community," or "Others will have trouble working for him. It's a matter of trust. You know he has been one of us," or "I'm suspicious, how did she get so far, so fast?"

Children injuring or killing other children represents the extreme of lateral violence. Consider a young teenage girl who beats or kills another girl because "she stole my boyfriend," a teenage boy struggling with his own sexuality who injures or kills another boy because "he walked like he was gay," or members of one street gang killing a member of a rival gang. In each case, the oppressor's image has been fully realized. As Pogo said, "We have met the enemy and he is us."

Internalization of Oppressor Tactics

Members of groups with a long history of being oppressed frequently internalize the values and goals of their oppressors. For example: a woman is furious at her husband's mistress; she holds her accountable, but not him. A member of an oppressed race attacks someone of the same race based on different religious beliefs. A person undermines a friend's success because she has received a promotion. An individual takes a stand that is against the best interest of coworkers because to do so grants that person more status, money and power. Perhaps most common is that a group you are in spends more energy on political infighting than on creating the mission, goals, objectives and ethics that will support the membership.

Political infighting within oppressed groups has destroyed many creatively conceived plans as well as led to further oppression for group members. "Political" arguments have interfered in the creation of well-thought-out plans for women's centers. Homosexuals—both male and female—fight amongst themselves over the right to be homosexual and the decision to marry or raise children. To some, one "politically" precludes the other. If you become a parent, do you have the "political" right to parent an opposite-sex child? If you marry, are you "buying into the system"?

Author Ruthann Robson speaks of exclusion based on the sex of her child (1997, p. 75). She stated that when she gave birth to a boy, she and her partner experienced the loss of some of their most loyal friends:

> *Inez said she could no longer come to meetings at our house because our house exuded maleness. Raquel told us she couldn't believe we simply didn't give up the male child for adoption. . . . Another proposed a rule that would bar all lesbians in any way participating in male-energized households from the group.*

When you begin to believe in only one right way or that others are expendable on the way to the top, or you find that your behavior reflects the attitude that "It's my way or the highway," you have internalized the values and the tactics of the oppressor. As one woman put it, "When I took a good look at myself, I realized that I had become the oppressive boss that I had both hated and feared."

Learned Helplessness

The concept of learned helplessness was explored in the preceding chapter. Briefly, when you have been rendered helpless by a more powerful other for a long period of time, you have learned that your success or failure is dependent upon something outside yourself, not your own actions or accomplishments.

This helpless stance can be set into motion by inescapable trauma, such as when an individual learns that nothing can be done to influence change. The motivation to escape decreases with the amount of time during which one has been subjected to the trauma. Uncontrollable reward also impairs motivation and leads to a state of learned helplessness, as if one is paid to stay helpless.

Oppressed groups are frequently the subject of both inescapable trauma and uncontrollable reward. Both lead to a helpless stance in life: "It's not going to matter anyway, so why try?" Some oppressed individuals become fearful of change and fearful that any actions on their behalf might result in further oppression. Again, the frustration and anger experienced results in a buildup of aggression that is often turned on others of the same group.

Release of Aggression

Oppressed communities exhibit many forms of violence: physical assault, verbal assault, putdowns and gossip. People who have been continually oppressed often feel helpless to fight back at the powerful oppressor, so the anger becomes directed laterally to members of their own group. When employee attacks employee, the real target of their anger is usually the oppressive boss. Saturday night brawls and gang violence are other examples of lateral violence.

Physical violence leaves scars on the outside and emotional violence leaves scars on the inside. One of the earliest symptoms of lateral violence is gossip. Those who engage in repetitive gossip often tell me they feel helpless. Someone does something that angers them. Perhaps they have felt put down, slighted, jealous or intimidated. They are terrified of conflict and feel helpless to express their feelings. Many have told me that "When I talk bad about the person I am upset with, I feel much better. I feel powerful."

Of course, if the individuals who are the targets of the gossip hear what has been said about them and are trying to establish honest communication and stop lateral violence, they may choose to confront the sources of the gossip. "Have I done something to offend you? I have heard that you are having difficulty with me and I'd like to straighten things out." The reply, "I don't know what you're talking about. I don't have any difficulty with you. Who told you? Was it . . . ?"

Gossip is a passive-aggressive form of violence that hurts, causes further alienation and isolation, and strengthens oppression. Many individuals feel afraid to reach out to others when they are depressed or suicidal, or they internalize agonizing trauma because of the fear that people would talk. One woman told me that she had been gang-raped when she was fifteen. She told a relative and was warned, "A lot of us have been gang raped in our youth. It's best not to say anything. It might get around and people will talk about you and your family."

Fear of Change, Fear of Choice

Many people work hard at healing the scars of oppression, but they feel discouraged. "I don't understand it. Just when I think we are moving ahead and breaking the cycle of oppression, we take many steps back and begin attacking one another again. Why?"

As difficult as it may be to understand, freeing oneself from oppression can be frightening. Consider the dilemma of the physically abused spouse. The act of breaking free from oppression can be particularly terrifying when a few individuals feel like they are standing alone. Sometimes the actions of those working toward liberation are threatening to those who fear further oppression. When the tyrannized turn on each other, the oppressor has little to do but fuel the fire.

A group that has been tyrannized for a long period of time

typically finds it difficult to change the internalized images of themselves as well as the internalized goals and values instilled by the oppressor. After years of learned helplessness, choice and responsibility can be frightening. It's a bit like being forced to kneel for a long period of time. Your legs eventually go numb. Once released from the oppressive position, you have difficulty standing and are afraid to walk without support for fear of falling.

Most prisoners of war will tell you that freedom can be terrifying. Individuals who have long been imprisoned or institutionalized yearn for freedom. When freedom is near, and the time comes for release, most are frightened. Many eventually find their way back to the security of the institution and to a dependency that has become familiar. Freedom becomes particularly fearful when no one has prepared those who have long been rendered dependent to again make choices and assume personal responsibility.

Their self-esteem has been injured through years of institutionalization and dependency. Fears of freedom and feelings of "failure" after being reinstitutionalized further injure their fragile self-worth. Once back in an institution, they deny their previous fears and again yearn for freedom.

Paulo Freire (1993, p. 30) explores the struggle for freedom and the dilemma of the oppressed:

> The conflict lies in the choice between being wholly themselves or being divided; between human solidarity or alienation; between following prescriptions or having choices; between being spectators or actors; between acting or having the illusion of acting through the actions of the oppressor; between speaking out or being silent, castrated in their power to create and re-create, in their power to transform the world.

Stopping Lateral Violence

The first step in stopping lateral violence is simply refusing to participate and compassionately educating participants whenever possible. When you refuse to participate in lateral violence, don't expect that others will be delighted and support you in your endeavors. You may not win popularity contests. Not engaging in putdowns and gossip can sometimes be like giving up an addiction. Active alcoholics, for instance, frequently feel threatened by friends who stop drinking. It makes them uncomfortable. Don't personalize negative reactions from practitioners of lateral violence.

Step two in stopping lateral violence is education. In order to continue tyranny, the oppressed must not be allowed to know and understand their oppressor's strategy. Many oppressed individuals have told me that learning about lateral violence was like being given a key to a prison.

One community leader commented, "It is sad to know that we've become contributors to our own oppression, yet it is freeing to know that once we are aware, we can stop hurting each other. We can use the angry energy we have directed toward each other to create solutions rather than further oppression. It will take time but it can be done."

It is extremely important to educate young people and to help them understand that violence directed at each other is misplaced. In one way or another, gang violence is the result of oppression. When youth are fighting turf issues over the sale of drugs, they are buying into the values of the dominant culture that "to have is to be." To attain immediate gratification, they kill members of their own race, while furthering the goals of the perceived oppressor. It is important to help gang members develop other goals and means of support.

In educating youth, everyone must understand that education is a participatory process. We learn from one another. Oppressive education assumes that the teacher knows everything and the student knows little to nothing: the "I know what's best for you" mentality. Young people have many lessons to teach as well as learn, and they can sometimes speak the truth more freely than their adult models.

One effective teaching method for helping youth break the cycle of oppression is the "Theater of the Oppressed," established in the early 1970s by Brazilian director and activist Augusto Boal. It is a form of theater of, by and for people that have been engaged in a struggle for liberation and who want to learn to fight against oppression in their daily lives.

The Theater of the Oppressed is a participatory theater where participants set the scene and act out oppressive events occurring in their own lives. An individual develops the scene of a recent experience of oppression. Others in the group are asked to play various roles. The individual who has developed the scene attempts to change the outcome that has resulted in feelings of powerlessness. When the protagonist is stranded, other members of the group are encouraged to take his place and continue attempts to find another way to attain liberation from the oppressive experience.

Reflecting life's reality, a guiding principal of the Theater of the Oppressed is that in attempting to change the outcome, one can't change the oppressor. The individual's personal power resides in changing the response to oppression.

The third step toward stopping lateral violence is understanding that freedom from oppression is not found in domination. Self-worth is not attained by limiting another's freedom, but from exercising choice and assuming personal responsibility for one's own actions, thoughts and behaviors. Becoming bigger does not require making someone else smaller. Aiding others in their personal fight for freedom can support your own freedom, just as lighting another's candle with your own creates more light, not less.

Your attempts at compassionate education may not succeed immediately. People carry burdens that we don't always see. Environmental and internal pressures influence the way we see, hear, think and act. Stressors also sometimes determine the energy we have to risk and grow. Others will change at their own pace. Their temporary regression is not a personal response to your efforts. As we say throughout this book, *don't personalize it!*

A fourth step in conquering oppression is developing learned optimism. Each individual must perceive the reality of oppression and believe that freedom from tyranny is obtainable. We need to break the cycle of learned helplessness. This is sometimes difficult because we can become discouraged when those we depend on for support take one step forward and two steps back. It will help to understand the fears inherent in recovering independence, choice and personal responsibility.

Oppression for most groups occurred over hundreds of years. Breaking the cycle of oppression isn't going to occur overnight. Sometimes we use the belief that "others are not changing" as an excuse to plunge back into our own learned helplessness. I have heard people say, "Nothing's going to work. People are just the same. Why should I keep knocking myself out?" When we adopt this belief, we allow ourselves to blame others for our increased sense of hopelessness, isolation and fear, as well as our unwillingness to continue risking. We sometimes stop examining ourselves and accepting responsibility for our own decisions, and we begin blaming, "It's not me, it's them."

Step five in combating lateral violence is developing zero tolerance, as many workplaces and organizations have done. In these workplaces, gossiping, belittling, putdowns and so on are violations of personnel policies and may result in disciplinary action if not stopped. One profession that has been historically oppressed and in which lateral violence has been epidemic is nursing. Many nursing organizations have become serious about stopping the painful effects of lateral violence and have been leaders in developing policies against its practice.

Everything we do can be a positive action toward actualizing a vision of a world without oppression and without enemies. We owe it to ourselves and we owe it to our children to believe this vision is possible.

"I'm Not Angry, but Get Out of My Way on the Highway"

"Hey! What's the matter with you anyway? That's my parking place! I saw it first!"

"Who do you think you are? Who taught you to drive?"

"I have the right-of-way here, you jerk! Get out of my way or I'll have to make you!"

"Hey, Gramps! Move it or park it! Some of us have places to go!"

These sounds are increasingly common on our roads and highways today. Losing one's temper behind the wheel has become so prevalent, we even have a name for it: road rage. Depending on the study cited, road rage has increased between 7 and 8 percent every year since 1990.

Stephanie Faul at the American Automobile Association (AAA) Foundation for Traffic Safety defines this behavior: *"Road rage is a violent assault that occurs as a result of a driving incident."* In road rage, a motorist makes a deliberate attempt to harm another person or their property. Psychologist Arnold Nerenberg of California is credited with coining the term.

Road rage has become so prevalent that many mental health professionals believe that it may be listed as a disorder in the next edition of the *Diagnostic and Statistical Manual of Mental Disorders* published by the American Psychiatric Association. Before we look at road rage more closely, consider these incidents, which are only a sampling of the types of behavior Americans risk facing whenever they drive a car:

- A man was driving along I-25 in Colorado Springs. He became so disturbed by a driver that repeatedly cut in front of him that he took out his gun and fired seven shots. One bullet hit the driver of the offending automobile in the head and killed him.

- In Utah, after a discussion about a fender bender, a driver gunned her engine and ran over the other driver, killing the individual.

- In Massachusetts, a driver flashed his high beams at another motorist who was perceived to be going too slow. The motorist in the lead car retaliated. After the two antagonized each other for a period of time they finally came to a stop. The slower driver retrieved a crossbow from his trunk and fatally wounded the other driver.

- In Washington state, a fifty-seven-year-old man killed a twenty-one-year-old college student because the student wasn't able to disarm his vehicle's alarm fast enough.

- A woman was shot because she accidentally hit another's Camaro.

- A small child was seriously wounded because her father accidentally cut off another motorist.

Our notion of "life out of balance" seems particularly appropriate here. Consider the efforts we put into automobile technology, and compare them to the (lack of) effort afforded to the emotional health of drivers. Cars are two-ton vehicles capable of speeds in excess of 100 miles per hour. They have been fully equipped by law with all kinds of safety features, including seat belts, side-impact beams and air bags. But what about the drivers? We put a lot of energy into making sure that enough physical protection is present to escape death in most automobile accidents. But what safety measures are in place to help prevent the operators of these imposing vehicles from becoming so enraged that they kill themselves or someone else? Many people are aiming their automobiles at other people as weapons of war, not to mention the large number of drivers who carry guns in their cars.

The list of road rage incidents seems endless and is growing daily. David K. Willis, president of the AAA Foundation for Traffic Safety, in a presentation on February 18, 1998, reported that a study by his foundation identified 10,037 road rage incidents between January 1, 1990, and the end of August 1996. He further stated that at least 218 men, women and children were killed as a result of these incidents and 12,610 people were injured. Reported incidents have grown steadily since 1990. Remember these are only the reported incidents. Many more incidents go unreported.

Although varying opinions exist on different aspects of the problem, road rage clearly crosses gender, age and economic lines. Some statistics indicate that mostly young males are responsible for road rage incidents; others believe that the behavior is more prevalent for people in their thirties; still others believe that the incidents are caused nearly equally by men and women from all age groups and walks of life including doctors, lawyers, ministers, blue-collar workers, welfare recipients. . . . If you also include screaming, hand gestures and threats as well as physical violence, the numbers and types of people that are afflicted with road rage expands, perhaps exponentially.

According to a study commissioned by the AAA in 1997, if you haven't felt or seen road rage in the last twelve months you are in the minority. Ninety percent of 526 motorists in that study said that they had experienced road rage within a year of the survey. Sixty percent said they had lost their temper. "Road rage" in this study was broadly defined as anger expression ranging from screaming and putting on the brakes inappropriately to using a weapon.

Another behavior of concern on our highways today is aggressive driving. Faul defines "aggressive driving" as "driving in such a manner to willfully endanger another motorist." AAA considers that aggressive driving is often the result of anger and frustration and that aggressive motorists operate vehicles without regard for their fellow drivers.

A congressional hearing in 1997 disclosed that aggressive driving was a factor in two-thirds of all traffic fatalities. Faul cautioned that aggressive driving refers to a behavior, not necessarily an attitude. The statistics could include the individual who gets behind the wheel when angry and drives a vehicle at a speed of one hundred miles per hour, the individual that is driving unsafely because a bee is in the vehicle, and everything in between. It is most likely that in the majority of cases, a driver is driving recklessly out of frustration and anger. Many individuals get in their vehicles intentionally when upset as a way of working out their anger or as a means of exiting a heated argument.

In an AAA-commissioned survey in 1995, 54 percent of the women and 63 percent of the men surveyed admitted to "aggressive driving." In a 1998 AAA aggressive driving survey of 942 adults beyond the age of eighteen, one-quarter of those questioned acknowledged that they engaged in aggressive driving. That suggests that out of nearly 180 million registered drivers in the United States, 45 million drive aggressively.

A 1998 news bulletin put out by AAA states:

> Of those who acknowledged engaging in aggressively driving, the most common reasons given for driving aggressively are

"running late" and "slow moving traffic in the left lane." Other factors cited included being angry over non-driving issues before getting behind the wheel, traffic congestion, and being angered by the actions of other drivers.

Judy told me that her husband Joe is an aggressive driver and has also engaged in road rage behaviors. Judy said that one of the things that bothers her most about her generally "mild-mannered" husband is that he is a "maniac" behind the wheel of a car. "He's like Jekyll and Hyde. He's the nicest man you'd ever meet most of the time. He never gets angry. When we get in the car he drives fast and constantly screams at other drivers. One time he actually got out of the car and banged on the hood of the car behind him because the person was honking. I was terrified. They guy in the other car retaliated and tried to run him over. I'm afraid one of these days he's going to get us all killed. How can a person change so completely just because he gets behind the wheel of a car?"

WHAT HAPPENS
BEHIND THE WHEEL OF A CAR?

"The Nicest Man"

Joe, to whom we were just introduced, was indeed one of the "nicest men you've ever met," on the outside. Inside he said he often felt like a "pressure cooker." He felt pressured at work and frequently internalized the anger he felt at his boss. At home, he also felt pressured, feeling that Judy and the kids made a lot of demands that he couldn't always meet adequately. He always smiled and was considered a "nice, easy-going guy" by work associates and friends.

As discussed in preceding chapters, anger isn't healthy unless it's expressed and released in ways that lead to appropriate action and resolution. Much like a balloon that is pumped too full of air, anger bursts out in inappropriate ways. Too often, built-up anger finds an outlet while its host is driving a vehicle. Joe didn't set limits or express healthy anger. Instead, his foot pressed far too hard on the gas pedal and his anger burst forth at fellow motorists. In the car, he felt in control: "I may not be the boss at work or home, but I've always felt that at least I was the boss on the highway."

Many people, like Joe, experience work situations that generate anger and at the same time prohibit release. People learn to suppress anger in relationships with friends and loved ones, fearing that if they express their anger they will be abandoned, go crazy or hurt someone. As we've discussed elsewhere, our culture tends to encourage inhibition of emotional displays. As day-to-day frustrations increase, suppression of anger can lead to the aggressiveness and the random violence we are observing on our roads and highways. Anger we hold toward people with whom we interact regularly, finds its outlet in anonymous bursts of rage against total strangers. Aggression is the emotion many people go to in response to frustration.

Some individuals on the road are, of course, angry all the time. They explode at the slightest provocation, particularly when their vulnerability is triggered. Although what we see on the outside is obviously not "a nice guy" but a "bully," this individual likely feels no more control or any more empowered than people who have difficulty releasing anger. People with an anger that doesn't subside but only changes in intensity have a "fire-breathing dragon" inside that both keeps others away from those vulnerable places as well as distances themselves from their own powerlessness.

People who suppress anger and live life behind a wall of invisibility ("Whatever you want," "Whatever you think") are as shame-bound as those with internal dragons. Individuals full of shame believe themselves to be "not good enough," "not perfect enough," "not strong enough," "unworthy." Behind the wheel of an automobile they can finally achieve the power and invisibility they seek. They can at last feel unseen. All the anger, powerlessness and hurt hidden under the shame finds a target in the form of an anonymous other.

The Anonymous Other

Aggressive drivers or perpetrators of road rage may ordinarily feel unable to stand up for themselves, but put them behind the wheel and they feel powerful and invincible. They might not be able to let a person close to them know how they're feeling, but they can release aggression on anonymous others. They also seem to feel justified in releasing their pent-up aggression on unknown individuals. Many who harm or kill others in road-rage incidents, for instance, defend their actions while expressing righteous indignation, "If he/she hadn't done X, then I wouldn't have done Y."

Many people believe themselves to be invisible in a car. I've seen people change clothes in a vehicle on a crowded highway as if they can't be seen. They experience the "freedom" of striking out at another and venting their anger and frustration without being "seen." Both parties in the transaction are anonymous. With anonymity seems to come a sense of power and a feeling that "I have nothing to lose, I don't know these people." Many studies indicate some people act far more antisocial when they think they are anonymous, when they don't feel they will "get in trouble." Their controls are external, not internal.

What Are the Reasons for Road Rage?

It's a Rush

The people we've been discussing to this point have some passive-aggressive qualities about their behavior. They seem to want to exercise their aggression without assuming any real responsibility for it. Some individuals, however, who are driving fast, gesturing and yelling literally like living in the fast lane. Their aggression is by no means disguised. They are addicted to the adrenaline rush of danger and anger.

As we noted earlier in the book, anger and fear feed on themselves, generating more of the same. The adrenaline produced is like an addictive drug that is harmful to your health. Not only can you kill yourself and take others with you, but the physical effects of constant fight or flight, as explored in chapter 1, can cause any number of physical illnesses. Many people seemingly addicted to adrenaline tell me that when they are not living on the edge they feel "barely alive." Living in the fast lane often camouflages a long-term, low-level depression in much the same way as do addictions to alcohol, drugs or food.

Now I Have Power

Many individuals tell me that they feel no power in their lives, that they are less and less able to influence many aspects of their day-to-day living:

"I don't talk to a person, I talk to a computer."

"There are more cars on the road, more construction, more traffic jams, more noise."

"My once-peaceful home is now surrounded by an apartment complex. They even cut down all the trees and I couldn't prevent it."

"I used to know my local grocer. If the food wasn't fresh or I didn't quite have enough money this week, I could talk to someone I knew or put it on my tab. Now my grocery store is part of a huge corporate chain. I feel insignificant."

"I used to have a family doctor who would spend time with me. Now I receive health care from an HMO (health maintenance organization). It's like they tell me what kind of treatment I'm allowed—never mind what I think I need."

"Keeping a job doesn't seem to relate to what a person does anymore. People are replaced in corporate takeovers or forced into early retirement. I used to feel a sense of pride in being able to support my family; now I've been 'downsized.'"

All of these individuals are expressing a sense of helplessness. They feel incapable of choice in an impersonal world. Michael Lerner refers to this feeling of insignificance as "surplus power-lessness." (Lerner, 1986, p. 5) He states, "Treating people badly is often the result of our previous surplus powerlessness, particularly our belief that everyone will always be hurting each other so we'd better do it first."

Unfortunately for other motorists, many people feel "power" behind the wheel of an automobile. These individuals feel like they are finally in charge: anonymous and surrounded by a ton and a half of metal. Their sense of helplessness, however, can be triggered by another motorist who will not comply with their need for control, their demands, their definition of appropriate road behavior or their standards. All of the pent-up powerlessness comes to the fore and they feel that they will lose face, self-esteem and status if their demands are not met. Many feel that they have the right to insult those who breach their set standards.

Some individuals actually feel they have the right to punish drivers who infiltrate their space. One woman who had recently lost her license told me, "I know it sounds crazy, but I can't stand another car in front of me. It's like I have to get ahead of it, have to be first. I'm realizing that I have felt last everywhere else in my life. At least I could be first on the highway. It shouldn't be worth all the speeding tickets I've received, but I didn't think about it at the time. I just reacted to this internal pressure to get in front of the car ahead of me. It's like I'm driven."

What to Do About Road Rage

Coupled with the following list of suggestions, you might find it useful to contact the AAA Foundation for Traffic Safety. They are currently one of the best resources on road rage and aggressive driving. They have information, studies and pamphlets on both types of behaviors, tips on their prevention and referral sources for those who practice these behaviors as well as their potential victims.

For Aggressive Drivers or Road Ragers

1. Understand your potential triggers: As with all difficulties related to unhealthy anger, it's important to understand situations that might trigger aggressive driving and road rage. For instance, the woman in the previous example learned that driving behind another car triggered powerlessness and her anger at feeling that she was always last. This trigger resulted in aggressive driving behavior. Common triggers may be someone following too close, honking, cutting you off, driving too slowly or taking the parking place you thought was yours. Understanding anger triggers can lead to feeling more in control and keeping you calmly in the driver's seat.

2. Learn to express your anger appropriately. As stated in other chapters, it's important to make friends with your anger and learn healthy expression. You might wish to seek out a support group or counselor to work toward healthy anger expression and develop tools for conflict resolution.

3. Don't get behind the wheel when you feel that your anger might be out of control. Drivers education courses used to show a movie entitled *Don't Drive When Driven*, and that's a good lesson to remember. A motor vehicle isn't a

tool to help you unload your anger: It's a means of transportation. Driving while high on drugs or alcohol is not safe, nor is it safe to drive when you're preoccupied or trying to process anger. The lives you save may be yours, your family's or mine.

4. Focus on other drivers as people, not anonymous objects. Taking out your anger on others is easier when they are depersonalized, but other drivers are people who sometimes make mistakes, just like you do. People occasionally drive poorly, just like you do. Someone, for instance, may simply have forgotten to signal when turning or pulling in the lane in front of you. Remember: don't personalize it. It is not a personal attack, it is a mistake—a dangerous one, but a mistake nonetheless.

5. Think of ways that help you to avoid or relieve stress while driving. A trigger for many people is highway congestion, particularly in terms of long commutes during rush hour or being caught in road construction. I now live in a section of Vermont where rush hour might be two cows and a duck, but when I lived in a Seattle suburb, commutes were often a nightmare. I learned that I would be much more relaxed if I changed my work schedule to avoid the congested rush hour whenever possible. For instance, I would leave for work at seven o'clock rather than eight. When I had to go during peak rush hour, I would call friends and carpool. I also would listen to the traffic reports on the radio and avoid congested roads whenever possible.

Because being late can also be one of my triggers, I also know that I should plan plenty of time for my commutes rather than putting myself in a situation where I have to rush.

Listening to calming music while driving helps relieve stress and tension. Others find it useful to listen to books on tape. One friend has a back massage cushion that she plugs into her cigarette lighter; another loves to sing while driving. Avoiding stressful situations and finding ways to safely remove stress are very important in preventing unsafe driving behaviors that are provoked by frustration and anger.

6. Learn to accept that not only are you not in control of the universe, you don't even control the piece of highway ahead of you. A very pertinent piece of wisdom is the Serenity Prayer written by Reinhold Niebuhr and used as one of the tools of Twelve-Step fellowships: "Grant me the serenity to accept the things I cannot change; the courage to change the things I can; and the wisdom to know the difference." This is a sound piece of advice regardless of your particular spiritual views. Many of us believe that we can control the actions of others and mold the universe into our own "perfect design." We can't. As we work toward changing the notion that we are in control, we might also work to regain the peacefulness found in humility.

7. Give other people a face, but not the power to control your actions. Learn to see other drivers as people going somewhere, just like you. These people are also experiencing stress, pain, hurt, disappointment and joy in their

lives. See them as human and also in control of and accountable for their actions, not yours. When a man pulls in front of you and you decide to punish him by hitting his bumper with your car, you are accountable for that reaction, not him. If you have difficulty sorting out accountability for incidents on the road, put a sign on your visor: "I am accountable for my choices and actions. I will not let an anonymous motorist ruin my day, or my life."

8. Driving aggressively or losing your temper does not make you more powerful; it could lead to increased powerlessness. How much power will you be exercising when you're sitting in jail or prison for acts committed in a fit of road rage? You could be making an out-of-control, split-second decision that could ruin your life and the lives of those you love. Take a deep breath and regain your personal power, as well as control over your speed, your car, your rage and your life.

9. If you find it difficult to stop directing your anger into aggressive driving or road rage, admit to yourself that you have a problem that could ruin your life. Seek help to regain control of your actions.

For Potential Victims

Remember that innocent people who make simple mistakes can be the unwilling victims of road rage. Keep the following tips in mind as you're in traffic, and try to practice them in encounters with other drivers.

1. Don't react to provocation. If necessary, pull over and let the out-of-control driver pass, or stop and yield the parking place you thought was yours. Compliment yourself on the choice you have made to empower yourself. You may have lost a parking space or a few minutes, but these days you may have saved your life.

2. Whenever possible, allow a lot of road space between yourself and erratic or obviously angry drivers. (Actually, you should do this as much as possible with safe drivers, too.)

3. If the offending driver will not leave you alone, drive to a police station or sheriff's office. Try to get the license number of the out-of-control driver's vehicle without being obvious.

4. Don't carry a weapon in your car.

5. Focus on the other driver as someone who has temporarily lost control for reasons unknown to you. You are not in a war zone and the rage is not directed at you personally.

6. AAA suggests locking your car doors when you are driving, knowing where you are going before you begin a journey and not making eye contact with a driver attempting to provoke you.

By using these suggestions, you could stop in a given instance the cycle of road rage that is engulfing our society. In so doing, you help fulfill one of the major responsibilities you have as a driver: making it home alive for your loved ones.

"I'm Not Angry,
but I'm Always Right"

*"Selfishness is not living as one wishes to live,
it is asking others to live as one wishes to live."*
—OSCAR WILDE

George was up early Sunday morning. He was careful not to wake Annette, quietly turning off her alarm on the bedside table. He wanted to surprise her by making a special brunch. He put fresh flowers in the vase on the center of the table and put out her favorite placemats. He prepared the foods she liked best: freshly squeezed orange juice and pancakes with hot, pure maple syrup. George knew that the week before had been difficult for Annette. Her parents had visited and she had knocked herself out, making everything perfect for them—yet they hadn't seemed to notice.

When Annette woke up, she immediately felt out of control. "Don't you know I like to get up early? Didn't you think I could have cooked breakfast? I had something already planned. I was saving those oranges for a cake. I wanted to cut the purple flowers for the table."

George and Annette ate breakfast in tense silence. After they had finished, George loaded the dishwasher and was told that he was loading it the wrong way. Finally George picked up the morning paper. Annette commented, "I just wanted to spend some time with you this morning, now you're reading the paper. I had the morning all planned out. I feel like our day together is ruined." She picked up her gardening shears and set out to cut the "proper" flowers for the table.

While in the garden, Annette felt the familiar feeling of intense loneliness and vulnerability, which was soon replaced by anger at George: "Didn't he think I could have cooked breakfast? Couldn't he at least talk to me instead of hiding behind his paper?" She then made a commitment to herself to make him understand that she was "right." He must understand that his behavior was "wrong" and act differently as proof of his love.

The need for one person to validate "rightness" over another person becomes a necessity for "right controllers" and can result in returning to the same issue for days until the need to be confirmed right by the offending party has been satisfied. Annette insisted upon talking late into the night about George's "inconsideration." She desperately needed an apology and his acknowledgment that she was right in order to release the anxiety that had been building in her all day. When George finally fell asleep, she experienced the desperation she usually felt under these circumstances. The abandonment she felt triggered her rage, "How could he just go to sleep like that when we haven't resolved our issues? Doesn't he care about me at all? I'll be up half the night while he just snores away." The feeling of abandonment and resulting fear and rage was real but had little to do with George.

Individuals like Annette feel a drive to be perfect, in control and "right." They don't merely argue, they fight for their lives. Their arguments have winners or losers and are centered on "right" and "wrong." The aim isn't to understand the other's point of view; instead answers are being prepared while they carefully listen for weaknesses in ideas to jump on, or for points that can be distorted in order to make the other look bad and feel guilty, "I had the day planned. Now the day is ruined."

When Annette and George married, George was still in college. He told me that he didn't want to live with Annette, let alone get married, until he had graduated and could contribute to their mutual support. "Annette wanted to get married before I finished my degree. She had already graduated and told me that she wanted to help me complete college without working so hard. I had been paying for my education by working nights and weekends. After we got married, however, she complained about needing to support us as well as about my 'poor' financial management skills. I could never do it 'right' enough. Even after I graduated, I still had no control over the money. Until the day I left, I got an allowance as if I was a little boy. My financial dependence during college was thrown in my face in every argument and used as proof of my ungratefulness."

COLLECTING RESENTMENTS

Some people are stamp collectors. When I was young, shoppers received green or gold stamps with groceries. The number of stamps received depended on how much you spent. The stamps were carefully pasted into "Green Stamp Books." When you saved enough books, you could trade in the books for desired items: seven books of stamps for a toaster, twenty books for a complete set of tools, etc.

Some individuals save unresolved issues or situations like green stamps: "You still haven't apologized for what you said to me the first time we met." "You'll never be able to make up to me for the time you . . ." "After all I've done for you, you continue to . . ." After saving enough of these resentments, the collection can be turned in on the right to be angry, as proof of one's "goodness" or even a guilt-free divorce. The hoarded resentments can serve as protection against further wounds to a vulnerable self. Several individuals I've worked with have been obsessed with proving that their ex-partners had affairs. This proof was needed to confirm that my clients were "good" all along and that the partners really were the "bad" people: "I knew it. I was right all along. The breakup wasn't my fault. All I want is for her/him to admit it."

The goal in right/wrong arguments is not to listen but instead to attempt to gain self-worth by being "right." The right-controller will use any tactic necessary in order to win. The unspoken message might be, "How could you do this to me after all I've done? I will demonstrate how cruel you are by the depth of my suffering. I will suffer, you will apologize and that will prove I'm right and, therefore, worthy of love."

Using Silence

Silence can also be a weapon to punish the other for perceived attacks or hurts. Sometimes silence about perceived wrongs grows from insignificant issues. I've known individuals who stop speaking to their partners for days over the right and wrong way to squeeze a tube of toothpaste. The ludicrous internal logic that the accuser uses in such a case is "If you insist upon squeezing the tube differently after I've told you the proper way, you're deliberately throwing it in my face that I'm wrong." The other's behavior is felt as a personal attack, and the cold shoulder can last for days until the other apologizes or makes up for the infraction.

Of course, the silent treatment is not healthy anger expression. This behavior can sometimes backfire and build into rage and abandonment anxiety if the other person appears unaffected by the silence. Silence is also ineffective communication. The person frozen out may have no idea that you're even angry.

Underlying Issues

Many arguments remain unresolved because the central focus of the quarrel is not the real issue. Unfulfilled needs lie under the desire to win the argument at hand. The internal monologue running in the head of the accuser may proceed along the lines of "I need you to share my view of reality to validate my own. If you don't share that view, that means I'm wrong, bad and not worthy of being loved. I must be in control so that I won't need you, feel hurt and vulnerable, or be dependent and abandoned again."

Instead of confronting painful issues, individuals who need to be right and in control unconsciously expect others to heal painful injuries from the past. As Harriet Lerner commented in *The Dance of Intimacy* (1989, pp. 17-18), "We become like the proverbial man who had too much to drink and lost his keys in the alley but looked for them under the lamp post because the light was better."

A partner's agreement to squeeze a tube of toothpaste in a specific site, load the dishwasher in a particular way or to put the correct flowers on the table isn't going to erase past pains of feeling unloved. A person cannot regain a positive sense of self by proving other people wrong. I ask couples I work with, "Does 'right' keep you warm at night?" The question is usually met with uncomfortable laughter and, of course, the answer is always "no."

Once gained, the words "You're right," or "Okay, I'll do it your way" seem sadly empty. There always exists the need for more validation, more power from partners and friends. Anger that's kept carefully hidden most of the time doesn't go away. The pain doesn't stop. Efforts on the part of partners, friends and others to heal beyond the emptiness can never be enough. The futile cycle continues.

Annette and George

Let's go back to Annette and George from the beginning of the chapter. Underlying Annette's self-righteous behavior is a need to be perfect enough to be loved. The righteousness and need to be in control is a defense against pain, humiliation, powerlessness and anger. She is terrified of being out of control. All expression of love must depend on her own efforts. She must be the perfect person worthy of love and George must act in a way that will undo the past, which is impossible. His wish to show how much he loved her by making breakfast and decorating the table backfired because inside she felt as though she didn't deserve it. She must find something wrong with it in order to remain in control and to continue to defend herself against the pain and years of built-up anger.

George, for his part, had a passive-aggressive style, "It seemed like I became more and more dependent. It was like I said to myself, 'I'll show you. You want to take care of everything, so take care of everything.'" He did less and less while Annette took on more responsibilities.

When I met George and Annette, they were separated. George had requested counseling many times only to be told that he should go alone because he was the problem. He said, "I finally got tired of being wrong, at never doing anything good enough to please her. I didn't feel that just being me was enough. I couldn't believe Annette was surprised when I asked for a separation. She was miserable, I was miserable."

Men and women who need to be in control and need to be right usually are surprised when their partners leave. Annette, for instance, was so caught up in her own dynamic that she couldn't see or hear George's pain and disappointment when his expressions of love were criticized or not accepted. Nor could she understand his need for independence. "Everything was going so well. I can't believe he wanted a separation!"

In Annette's early life, the focus of care in the family centered on a mentally challenged younger brother. Annette was expected to be a "good girl" and ask for little. As with so many children that lack attention, Annette established the belief early that if she could be good enough, model the correct behavior and always do the right thing, she could achieve the love and attention she desperately needed. By the time of her marriage, she was still attempting to achieve unmet needs and began to do so through her husband. In Annette's case, her parents were preoccupied with another sibling. Other preoccupations in a marriage—with alcohol, drugs or other addictions; with each other; with issues in life—can also produce children that strive to be perfect enough to be loved. This dynamic develops in many children who have been sexually abused as well, when the nonoffending parent is passive or unable to protect, or appears to have chosen a partner over the abused child. Such children feel at fault for the abuse and may set out to prove that they can still be good enough to be loved.

In some cases, individuals who protect themselves by always wanting to be right develop patterns of repeatedly leaving relationships. Their fear that they can't change their partners is so intense that, lacking results, they must leave. They still feel empty. They interpret the feeling of emptiness to mean they're not in love anymore. They experience feelings of anger towards their partners for not loving them enough to fill the emptiness.

Oddly enough, if those same partners leave them first, they will fight to get them back in an addiction-like manner. Each individual again enters the cycle feeling that "if only I can get that person back, I will be loved at last." Interestingly enough, if the

individual has a child, too much attention may be unknow... ,
focused on the partner to the exclusion of the child, creating the
same potential dynamic for the next generation.

Right-controllers tend to be tremendously loyal in work relationships and in friendships. Feeling unappreciated or criticized,
however, can result in their ending friendships or leaving jobs. In
order to do so, they must first justify their leaving with full books
of stamps that prove that they are right and wronged. These circumstances are usually accompanied by little communication,
and friends or individuals in the workplace frequently haven't
known that anything is wrong. Upon an "ex-friend's" insistence,
one right-controlling woman presented proof that her friend
didn't care. When listing the stamps saved in anger, the right-
controller reported that she had counted the number of times
each had gone to the other's house over the years. She concluded
that if her friend "really cared about the friendship," the visits
would have been more equal.

FOR THOSE WHO
"NEED TO BE RIGHT" IN RELATIONSHIPS

Before discussing what can be done to break the right-
controlling cycle, let's review the characteristics and probable
causes of this type of personality:

- Often the need to be right is accompanied by the
  unconscious belief that if you are really good enough you
  can attain the love you so desperately want. Self-
  righteousness does not result in more connection with

others or increased self-worth. Instead, the more likely outcomes are further isolation and increased feelings of emptiness.

• The drive behind the need to be right is energized by a tremendous amount of pain, shame and anger. Low self-esteem, hurt and angry feelings cannot be relieved by feigning perfection or by having other people acknowledge that you are right.

As a right-controller, you may unconsciously seek out individuals whom you perceive need you, have a passive-aggressive style, or are shaming. You may not even be attracted to individuals whom you don't need to chase or who aren't dependent on you. A key to change can be recognizing this cycle early, allowing you to begin to operate on choice rather than impulse and past history. Consider these steps for breaking the cycle of these forms of unhealthy relationships:

1. Recognize that you are trying hard to convince the other of your goodness.
2. Realize that you are feeling obsessed with the relationship (thinking about the person constantly, waiting by the phone, developing interests that allow you to have greater contact with the individual, feelings of desperation).
3. Recognize that your self-esteem is beginning to depend on the other's attention. The following actions should act as triggers for this knowledge:
   — Feeling good when he or she calls and depressed when there is less contact.
   — Feeling disappointment or anger at the other's behavior and not being able to express the feelings for fear of rejection.

— Feeling that you have the ability to change the other person into someone who will love you in a way you want to be loved.

— Feeling greater emptiness shortly after a commitment is made in the relationship.

— Finding more and more fault with the other's behavior and your increasing need to be right.

— Recognizing that you are beginning your "stamp collection."

— Feeling more energized by the other's rejection than by their commitment.

— Finding yourself getting angry at positive attention.

— Feeling like the other is not living up to your expectations and finding yourself disappointed and "falling out of love."

— Wanting to exit the relationship or developing a vague awareness that you are pushing the other away.

Keep in mind that this last step is sometimes an attempt to regain the energy that is felt at the beginning of the relationship through the act of rejecting them and then fighting to rekindle the original emotions: "making them love me."

4. Develop the awareness that making a mistake doesn't mean you are unlovable: It merely means you made a mistake, and there's no shame in that. Making mistakes is one of the best teaching tools we have.

5. Remember that it's not possible to change another person directly. It never has been. If you feel isolated and alone today, only you can change the situation. Your partners cannot repair the past. They can, however, be supportive in

your efforts or perhaps even lead by example.

6. Counseling is an important part of the process of healing. Choose the right modality for you: individual, group, couples or family counseling.

7. Recognize your separateness and confront the fantasy that "If I only try hard enough and be perfect enough, I can make people love me." Your happiness and self-esteem do not depend upon the validation of others. Through therapy you can begin to confront your anger, vulnerability and old pain.

When choosing a counselor, be sure to select one who is able to confront you in a kind and compassionate way, providing you with the honest mirror discussed earlier in the book. Seeking out counseling can be the beginning of the healing cycle. If you're thinking that your therapist will be an ally in changing your partner, you're in therapy for the wrong reason. If the therapist wants to help you change your partner, as much as this justifies your internal monologue, you might choose another therapist, because you're only delaying your own healing.

FIGHTING FOR OUR LIVES— THEM AND US

In society today, our need to be right extends far beyond close relationships. In our broader culture, we do not seem to have healthy discussions but rather arguments that require winners and losers. We seem to need to make others wrong in order to have our own point of view. We frequently respond to another's ideas with criticism. The world ends up being divided between *them* and *us*, and little attention is paid to points of commonality or agreement.

As stated by Deborah Tannen in *The Argument Culture:* "The argument culture urges us to approach the world and the people in it in an adversarial frame of mind. It rests on the assumption that opposition is the best way to get anything done. Best way to begin an essay is to attack someone, best way to show you're thinking is to criticize." (1998, p. 3)

I recently witnessed a heated argument between two acquaintances regarding President Clinton's acknowledgment of an inappropriate sexual relationship with a White House intern. Both people regarded his sexual conduct as inappropriate yet they barely acknowledged agreement on that issue. The point they became heated over was whether he should be impeached.

One individual felt the president's sexual conduct was between him and his family and had nothing to do with his ability to serve in the office, while the other person believed Clinton's behavior was reprehensible enough that he should be forced to leave office. The two became more and more entrenched in their own beliefs as the argument progressed. At one point they began personal attacks on one another. That was enough for me. I asked, "Aren't you both entitled to your own points of view?"

They looked at me as if I were crazy, ignored me and kept on fighting. One accused the other of being immoral. The other said, "How can you be so judgmental? You've had affairs and told the person you had the affair with not to tell." The reply, "I'm not the president."

These two individuals are currently not speaking to one another. The issues didn't seem to be as important as who was right and who was wrong. The degree of anger expressed was far more than the situation warranted. They seemed to be fighting and defending as if their lives depended upon winning.

ANONYMITY

In some cases, personal contact is not even necessary to prolong heated opposition. Work associates often become furious because of a memo. In one situation to which I was privy, the contents of a memo led to battle lines being drawn between work associates in a four-person office. The feud went on for months. Why were they sending memos anyway? People were sending e-mail and memos to other people at desks not twenty feet away.

Technology has allowed us to become more impersonal with one another. We say things in memos and through e-mail and voice mail that we may never say face to face, and the effect of the criticism seems far more lasting. The recipient of the hurtful message is more likely to become antagonistic and less likely to request personal contact. Instead, people seethe in isolation, gather forces for the battle, or respond with equal or more antagonism through the same impersonal mode of communication.

Tannen comments on our growing anonymity, as expressed in the incidents of road rage explored in the previous chapter: "If the anonymous driver to whom you've flipped the finger turns out to be someone you know, the rush of shame you experience is evidence that anonymity was essential for your expression and experience of rage." (1998, p. 239)

MORAL AND RIGHTEOUS ANGER

All of us at one time or another have felt outrage at what we judge to be morally wrong. For instance, we would condemn the senseless killing of 168 people in the Oklahoma City federal building bombing or the abuse of children. There is a world of difference, however, between occasional outrage at wrongdoing and the morally angry extremist who believes he or she has found *the* right answer and the one true way. Such individuals feel that they not only know what's right for them but for everyone else as well. They believe they have the right to encourage followers to be angry at anyone with a differing opinion. Many interrupt others in conversations, "I don't believe you said that! Surely you don't really believe that? How can you possibly believe that? What's wrong with you?" Some people maintain that they have the right to eliminate people who do not share their opinions or to kill to bring notice to their perceived wrong in a situation.

Believing abortion is wrong is one thing, but burning down a medical clinic where abortions are practiced, or killing a physician who performs abortions, is quite another story. A person may believe that homosexuality is wrong, but that opinion does not come with the right to beat up lesbians or gay men, or to shame them or deny them employment based solely on sexual orientation. A person has the right to pray in a manner of their own choosing but does not have the right to eliminate nonbelievers or force them to adhere to other belief systems.

Fanatics

Some extremists believe that they have the right to decide what's best for a group of people or even all of society. These personalities are often referred to as fanatics. Consider four such *fanatics* in recent history:

- Adolf Hitler believed he was part of a superior race.

- Jim Jones believed he was the one true leader of a new society.

- David Koresh believed he was the emissary of God, the new Christ.

- Marshall Herff Applewhite believed that a spaceship following behind a comet would take the "chosen" to a new world.

These men not only held their own extremist beliefs, but they had the personal power to persuade others to discard their own choices and inhibitions and blindly follow the one with The One True Answer.

Fanatics believe themselves to hold ownership to the one and only "truth," and in possessing this knowledge they imagine themselves as invulnerable. They believe that they alone are right and have the power to magically change the world into a paradise worthy of their rule. They believe themselves, therefore, to have absolute knowledge, power and authority.

Most of these individuals live at the far end of narcissistic disorders, tending toward paranoia. They are arrogant, grandiose and insensitive to the feelings of others. Narcissists are self-involved and far more concerned with how they appear than how they feel. They repressed feelings long ago and must deny feelings that challenge the images they strive to achieve.

A large gulf exists between the images fanatics hide behind and their true selves. For instance, they typically believe themselves to have extraordinary powers, when in fact they experienced deep humiliation and powerlessness most of their young lives. The fanatical image that they've created protects them from experiencing the powerlessness, fear and self-hate hidden behind the false self.

True self-acceptance is lacking in fanatics. The image is only a facade. Similar to the right-controllers, they need others who will applaud and admire them in order to feed the false self. Fanatics crave devotees to give them the power and control they desperately need to keep their masks in place. Denial and repression of their true feelings of fear, powerlessness and self-hate are crucial.

People who consider themselves omnipotent resemble the queen in Disney's *Snow White and the Seven Dwarfs* who needed a mirror that would continually reassure her of her power and verify that she truly was the "fairest of them all." Fanatics need others to be the dishonest mirror that feeds their projected image of omnipotence: "Mirror, mirror, on the wall . . . who's the most admired and powerful of them all?" Of course because the façade does not have a supply of self-worth to feed it, any amount of adoration and power is never enough. Their feelings of omnipotence must be reinforced constantly.

Fanatics channel all of their aggression toward a faceless enemy conveniently characterized by the "imperfections" they themselves have been accused of possessing: selfishness, sexuality, homosexuality, laziness, weakness, vulnerability, stupidity, heathenism, promiscuity, dependency, etc. Rage that was once directed toward the fanatic as if he or she were inhuman becomes directed at others whom the fanatic deems inhuman.

Alice Miller, in *The Untouched Key* (1988), compares Hitler's family to a "totalitarian regime" under the control of dictators who emphasized obedience and strict control. Young Adolf couldn't take joy in playfulness or creativity. He was not allowed to question or have his own ideas, thoughts, needs or emotions. Hitler's father exercised arbitrary power and brute force in attaining discipline and control. As a child, Hitler was punished cruelly and relentlessly for any infraction of his parents' wishes. He was not allowed to disobey.

Hitler's use of arbitrary control and power in the Third Reich mirrored the family system in which he was raised. Ordinary citizens in the Third Reich were not permitted to question a decision made by the state or the Gestapo. Those who tried were tortured or killed. Brute force represented the ultimate power, and it provided its own "justification" for "maintaining order" and for the "legality" of its crimes. (Miller, 1988, p. 51)

Hitler identified with the aggressor and treated the people he led as he had once been treated: insensitive to needs, ideas or human emotions. It is believed that Hitler's grandfather was Jewish, and Hitler would fly into rages whenever his father's Jewish hometown of Spital was mentioned. He focused his aggression on all Jewish people, crediting them with the characteristics that he was cruelly and arbitrarily punished for as a child.

Fanatics experience blind rage whenever their vulnerability, powerlessness or self-hate is triggered. Any challenge to their power and image or any breakthrough of their original fear and vulnerability yields an uncontrollable anger that is often murderous and which does not end until it is completely exhausted.

FOLLOWERS OF FANATICS

Sadly our society sometimes has to deal with the fanatically, morally righteous individuals such as Adolf Hitler, David Koresh or Jim Jones, or the type of fanatic who burns down an abortion clinic, church, gay bar, or Jewish synagogue. What might be less easy to comprehend, though, are the thousands of people who follow such extremists. What could possibly motivate individuals to commit mass murders or suicides; to believe in only one right answer, one correct religion or one "chosen" race; or to succumb to the rantings of fanatics?

The answer to this question is complex, and not one answer is correct for all groups. First, fanatics can appear sincere, charming, concerned and intelligent. People are usually more susceptible to their charisma, power and promises during times of social, economic or spiritual decline. Followers are searching for faith, hope, inclusion and the promise of a secure and loving community. As stated by Haynal, Molnar, and De Puymege (1983, p. 71):

> The danger of fanaticism likewise stalks groups threatened with social decline, either for family reasons, following the loss of the father, for instance, or because of economic circumstances. The result is bitterness and aggressiveness, corresponding to feelings of rejection. Those injured by life become susceptible to the demands of the socially oppressed with whom they can identify, even if they have not necessarily experienced the same suffering. Their narcissistic wounds make them candidates for fanaticism.

The charming fanatic seductively offers individuals a sense of importance, a hope for a better world, relief from the constraints of a punitive conscience, a target upon whom to release pent-up aggression, love, meaning in life, belonging and attachment to others, hope, the promise of infinite peace, and, for some, a way out of seemingly endless emotional pain.

One follower who had been orphaned as an infant said, referring to her time in a fanatical religious sect, "I don't think I've ever felt a sense of peace. I've probably felt unworthy and unloved all my life. I also was the person others, including adults, always depended on. He (the charismatic founder of the sect) originally offered me love, the promise of internal peace and a relief from emptiness. I was given a family complete with a 'dad' who would take care of me. It sounds strange but it was a relief to be dependent and told what to do every moment of the day. Of course the fantasy was much different than the reality."

Many people want to believe that someone can give them an "ideal world," particularly those who have felt exclusion or a need to escape from this world. They want to believe in the power of another to transform their lives.

Followers of fanatics believe in things that most would find absurd. The notion that a spaceship is following a comet and has been sent to retrieve the spirits of a chosen few would seem ridiculous to most individuals. Those that believe do so because they want to believe, just as little children want to believe in Santa Claus. They want to believe in magic and magical solutions. As grownups, they have lost, for whatever reason, belief that they are responsible for their own lives and have the power and influence to affect their destiny. These individuals want to feel special and important. They find importance, if not omnipotence, in being one of the chosen few.

Once under the influence of a fanatical leader, individuals are frequently required to give up all personal belongings and interests. They are often not allowed to associate with "nonbelievers," including family members. Their daily lives are controlled and sometimes, as was the case in Hitler's Germany, they are punished for independent thoughts or actions. One is not allowed to place trust in one's own judgment. Individuals must comply with the whims and wishes of the fanatical leader. Some have said they feared retribution, not only for themselves, but their families as well if they didn't follow the rules or dared to question the leader's beliefs or requirements. Many members of extremist sects have related stories of emotional and physical abuse.

While under the influence of fanatical leaders, most individuals soon lose any remaining vestige of personal power or self-esteem and become increasingly dependent. As we've seen throughout this book, these are the exact seeds of an anger that is cyclical and which becomes increasingly difficult to resolve.

"I'm Not Angry, but I'm Going to Show *You* Who's Boss"

"Power can be seen as power with rather than power over, and it can be used for competence and cooperation, rather than dominance and control."

—ANNE L. BARSTOW

I remember the last time I saw my father. He appeared almost lifeless in a bed on the ward of a military hospital. There were many other men close to his age in the same room. I almost didn't recognize him. I remember telling my brother, "He's not in there." In his illness my father was only a shadow of the man I remembered. I thought, could this be the father that caused so much fear in my young life, the big, tough Marine that glorified war and told war stories most nights when he was drunk? Could this be the man that kept me awake nights fighting with my mother, or the man that would tell my brother and I not to cry when he beat us with extension cords or his Marine Corps belt? He was a man that used his fists and sometimes shot target practice out in our backyard with the same gun our mother used to kill herself.

My father at times was a gentle man. My aunt told me he was always gentle and kind to her when he was a boy. He lied about his age and joined the Merchant Marines at fourteen and then enlisted in the Marine Corps. My father was fighting in World War II when he was not much more than a boy, sending his checks home to support his mother and some of his younger siblings.

After the war, he was never the same. The gentle boy was now an often-violent alcoholic. As I looked around the hospital room at others like my father, dying too early, I wondered how many had been violent in their homes. I questioned how many had, like my father, acted out every battle of the war with their families and how many had nightmares each night. I wondered how many of the men dying on that ward had never been "de-warred" and instead had been sent home to teach to their families the lessons they had been taught in boot camp and on the battlefield.

I remembered my father shaming my brother, frequently calling him a "sissy" or teaching him to be "tough," to "be a man." I was told that when my brother was a toddler dressed in a white outfit, my father had put him in a mud puddle telling him to "get dirty. . . . Don't be a sissy."

Many veterans not only suffer from post-traumatic stress disorder, but also have internalized the image of the military that "might makes right." That image and the patriarchal values that typically accompany it, through emotional and physical violence, can be passed down for several generations. A number of individuals I have met can trace domestic violence in their families back to the Civil War.

As stated by James Gilligan, "My father was caught in a cycle of generations of violence that played itself out in our family as it had, indeed, in the very land on which we were living, a land purchased with the blood of the natives whom we displaced." (1997, p. 15) The violence we practice is not born within us, but rather more often is a behavior learned from our adult models.

LEARNED BEHAVIOR

Violence is learned behavior. Most boys are socialized to be aggressive and dominant. The values of power and control are often reinforced daily by coaches, parents, television shows, movies, the military, the music industry and so on.

My oldest son still remembers the shaming by a junior high soccer coach who called the boys "sissies" if they didn't win and made them run laps until they collapsed. One father "accidentally" broke his son's arm because he didn't attend the goal well enough. I saw a mother slap her son in the face because he didn't hit the ball in a Little League game. A gym teacher drilled holes in the wall between the boys' and girls' showers and gathered the boys to watch the girls as they undressed. Still another coach in a junior high basketball camp would regularly call the boys "suburban jump-shot faggots."

In the small town of Glen Ridge, New Jersey, on March 1, 1989, a group of adolescent males raped an intellectually challenged schoolmate with a broomstick and a baseball bat. The boys were the top athletes of the school and were glorified by the town from the time they first showed talent in sports. According to author Bernard Lefkowitz in *Our Guys,* the jocks in Glen Ridge were filled with self-importance. Community members protected them and blamed the victim, saying that she was "promiscuous" and must have "asked for it." The boys were protected and esteemed even after the town was aware of the brutal rape. She was also not the only young woman to be violated by the town's promising young athletes. "Although what happened to Leslie was an act of singular cruelty, she was not the only young woman to be misused in Glen Ridge's gung-ho culture. The indifference in the community to how girls were being treated by young males, especially favored athletes, stole the childhood innocence away from the most vulnerable young women. . . ." (1997, p. 491)

Violence is frequently glorified in the media as well. Rarely a day goes by that some form of violence isn't the lead story in newspapers, on local radio stations or on TV, because violence sells. The general public becomes desensitized to violence for three reasons:

1. We are continually exposed to senseless violence. The number of gruesome and gory details are steadily increasing in the presentations of violence.

2. Our exposure to violence lacks the firsthand, personal impact that is experienced in the lives of victims and their families.

3. The general public is being exposed to operant conditioning techniques that are the same procedures used to train soldiers to kill in the Vietnam War. This will be explored fully in the next chapter.

The music industry routinely promotes male dominance, violence toward women and the glorification of drugs. One of my sons worked in an inpatient facility for youth with drug and alcohol addictions. He was horrified by the music the youth were regularly playing and let them know that he would not tolerate music that taught negative values. He explained that the lyrics promoted violence toward women and glorified drug and alcohol abuse, which were exactly the behaviors the facility was trying to condition the children against. He told the youth that when he heard the music he was insulted by the disrespect it showed for his mother, his sister, his aunties and his partner. Consider the teachings in the lyrics from Snoop Doggy Dogg's "Doggystyle" where women are devalued and repeatedly referred to as "bitches."

The graphics for that particular album also include a cartoon with a scene glorifying drugs and domestic violence. Although the cartoon depicts dogs, the artist portrays them to resemble adult men and women. The language is extremely explicit so I will describe it rather than quote it directly: A highly sexualized female dog is told that she is not allowed to stay in the dog house because she didn't bring "chronic" (marijuana). She flies all the way to Jamaica to get the male dog some "chronic ganja." He becomes angry because he can't find paper to roll a joint. She immediately offers to get papers for him. He calls his "homey" instead to bring some. Later in the cartoon he screams that the chronic is no good and violently kicks her out.

Women are characterized in lyrics and in the cartoon as either "bitches" or "hos." The parental advisory on the CD cover warns of explicit lyrics, yet this performer's music has on occasion topped the sales charts. Parents often have no idea what their children are listening to. One parent told me, "I can't even understand the words in the lyrics today. It sounds like so much noise to me. I guess I need to take the time to listen to the music with my children." My son talked to the youth and their parents, offering to assist them in the selection of popular music that offered positive messages; one example he gave was the lyrics of songs by the rap group Arrested Development.

Pretty posters with positive messages often cover the walls of schools and teen centers, but the violent messages of aggression, sexism, control and power delivered by adult models in the media—via popular music, video games, TV shows and movies—override and overwhelm the more understated messages displayed where children are educated.

DOMESTIC VIOLENCE

Another aspect of learned behavior is the cycle of violence that too many families experience at home. Even for families in which domestic violence is nonexistent, consider the items they see and hear on the news: An infant is beaten almost to death because it won't stop crying; a child is pummeled because he spills his milk;

a young wife is choked because she served her partner a macaroni-and-beef casserole with the wrong kind of cheese; an elderly woman is locked in the basement while her adult children live off of her Social Security checks. You might not even want to consider how many other stories we either don't hear about because of the fear of the abused or that don't come to light because of the craftiness of the perpetrators.

Thousands of children are neglected, abandoned, sexually exploited, shot, scalded, burned, set on fire, beaten, strangled, drugged, thrown out windows, suffocated, or raped by their fathers, mothers, aunts, uncles, cousins, baby-sitters, grandparents, or other adult models every day. Remember the importance of modeling we've referred to in this book and consider the implications for society of the manner in which many of these children will grow up.

Thousands of women are strangled, kicked, punched in the face, burned, threatened, scalded, hit, shot at, raped or suffocated daily by male partners and at times by female partners. Emotional abuse is always part of domestic violence as well.

Thousands of elderly daily are tied to beds and chairs, hit, punched, kicked, choked with food, strangled, raped or confined to basements by their adult children, partners or caretakers.

Although not as common and the balance of power is far from the same, I have treated men that have been scalded with liquid or hot food, burned, or regularly hit and kicked by partners as well, without retaliating violently.

Domestic violence also occurs in same-sex couples and should not be minimized in gay and lesbian relationships because the power seems more equal: man to man or woman to woman. I have treated women that have been severely abused by their female partners—stalked, intimidated with weapons and terrified to leave. Similar dynamics occur in some relationships between gay men.

Many incidents of violence toward the elderly, women and children are witnessed by neighbors or other community members who may be shocked, but who do nothing. For instance, a woman's abusive partner tied a rope around her neck and dragged her along the cement floor of a mall parking lot while bystanders watched and never intervened.

Domestic violence is a national epidemic, but unlike polio or smallpox, domestic violence has not always been viewed with the same focused worldwide effort as other deadly epidemics. Contrary to the beliefs of many people, domestic violence is not about anger; rather it is about displays of power and control that are sometimes fueled by long-standing internalized rage, powerlessness and terror.

Rick's violence trigger was vulnerability and powerlessness. Any time feelings of powerlessness were triggered in him, he would strike out violently against his wife and children, and occasionally against other men in barroom brawls. The trigger could be his child's illness, his infant son's cry, not being able to pay the bills, the fear in the eyes of his wife or children, the death of a relative, etc.

Rick finally faced consequences for his violence when he severely injured another man in a bar fight. He served some jail time and was required to attend an alcohol program as well as an anger-management group. He had completed both programs and had been sober for some time when he again hit his wife.

Everyone, including Rick, was surprised that—"stone-cold sober" and after countless teachings in anger management—he still struck out violently. But Rick's violence was not about drinking or anger, it was about power, control and terror at his own vulnerability.

Rick had been raised in a domestically violent home where he frequently witnessed his father beating his mother up physically and emotionally. "He also punched my brothers and me when we didn't get out of his way. He always let us know how useless we were." When Rick was seven, his father asked his family to join him in the back yard. He was holding a gun aimed at his family. Rick said he was terrified that his father was going to shoot them all. He instead turned the gun on himself, shooting himself in the head.

At one point in his treatment, Rick was able to remember the terror and powerlessness he felt as a little boy. He became aware that after his father's suicide, he had immediately stopped feeling, "I don't think I have felt anything for years. My mother always told me I was going to be just like my dad, and maybe I am. I'm jealous of my wife like he was. I shame and hit my wife and kids like he did. I was a drunk like he was. I want it to be different. I don't want to come to the same end he did. I don't ever want to put my wife and children through that particular hell." Rick became aware that his trigger to violence was powerlessness. To respond to the trigger, rather than allowing the feelings, he immediately bypassed vulnerability and struck out violently. He began drinking at an early age and was constantly in one fight after another, although prior to his last bar brawl he had no criminal record. The alcohol lessened his inhibitions but did not cause his violent behavior. Like many abusive partners, Rick had for many years blamed his violence on a combination of alcohol and his wife's behavior. Unlike many others, Rick was highly motivated for treatment, which made it easier to break through his denial and rationalizations.

Sandee, Rick's wife, also grew up in an abusive family. Although her father never hit her, he physically abused her mother and emotionally abused the whole family. She remembered many nights hiding under the bed with her brothers and sisters while her father was beating her mother. "I guess on some level, I believed my mother caused the violence toward her. I thought if she'd just shut up Dad wouldn't hit her. I thought she provoked him. I promised myself as a wife I would never demand, nag or get angry. I didn't do those things and got hit anyway."

Sandee also remembered times that she would be beaten by her mother. "It was almost like the violence just moved down the line: My dad hit my mother and after a while, my mother started hitting me. Sometimes my older brother would get hit by my father and would hit my younger brother. None of us talk to each other now. I feel very proud, though, that I've never hit any of my children, although sometimes I have called them down when I'm really frustrated. I have to stop that. I'm only now learning to be a parent."

Like many abused partners, Sandee left once in the relationship. "My oldest daughter was a baby and he hit me because she wouldn't stop crying. When he was at work, I packed us up and went to my sister's. He found us and threatened my life if I ever left him again. Then he apologized and worked really hard for a short time to prove to me that it wasn't going to happen again. I wanted to believe him. Of course it did happen again. I never left after that one time. I believed he would keep his promise and kill me if I did. The fact that I had left him once came up many times when he was letting me know who was boss."

Sandee's experience is not uncommon. Many victims of domestic violence have left only to return out of fear or belief that their partner has permanently changed.

TO VICTIMS OF DOMESTIC VIOLENCE

Domestic violence is not the fault of the abused. All relationships have conflict. Many family members have difficulty communicating and say things at times that they wish they hadn't. There is no conflict, argument, difference of opinion or behavior, however, that justifies either physical violence to another individual or the destruction of their personal possessions. There is also no justification for emotional abuse. Emotional violence—in the form of putdowns, intimidation, limiting the personal freedom of a partner, threats, stalking, public humiliation or continual unsupported accusations—always accompanies physical violence.

Try to remember also that domestic violence is not about anger. An abusive partner with access to the range of emotions, including healthy anger, wouldn't be physically violent. Domestic violence is about power, control, fear and a need to express vulnerability.

In situations of domestic violence, the violent partner will most likely apologize after hurting you. The apology or promises that it will never happen again may sound sincere, even if you have heard them before. Abusive partners have systems of rationalization and deny the seriousness of their behavior. A violent domestic partner who stops violent behavior without external consequences and treatment is the rare case.

Victims of domestic violence should develop a supportive network that might include friends, understanding family members, spiritual counselors, etc. For battered women, there are usually trained advocates in your area that can assist you in making decisions that are right for you. They can help you find resources including safe housing, help with children, financial resources and legal support, as well as develop safety plans. When you know that violence is escalating, you should know resources and safe exit routes from your house, and have access to survival kits that have been left with a friend or neighbor. Survival kits should include money, clothing, documents such as birth certificates, etc. Do not leave your survival kit inside your home. Most states have toll-free numbers that you can call. Your communication is confidential.

Domestic violence is against the law and many police departments are better trained than they have been in the past to deal with it. Know the emergency numbers. Remember, laws have changed.

If your partner is directing violence toward a child, call for help immediately. If you have, or are concerned that you will become abusive to your child, call for help immediately in this case also. Work with your advocate to assist you in ensuring the safety of your children. This may mean arranging "time out" for yourself. If you have been emotionally or physically abusing your children, you must seek help and begin counseling now. Remember, violence is never justified.

As the abused person, only you can decide when it is safe to leave a violent relationship. Sometimes an abusive partner becomes more dangerous after you have left. Be sure to establish an effective safety plan. When you know you're safe, it may be important to seek counseling for yourself and your children in order to work through the effects of post-traumatic stress that violence, grief, loss and shame cause. Your counselor also may assist you in developing future goals and plans. You may have grown up in a violent environment where abuse was normalized. Recognizing repeating patterns that you may have developed over the years will help you regain self-esteem, personal power, and may aid you in effective parenting.

Many of us grew up with models who did not know how to resolve conflicts effectively. It is important to develop communication and conflict resolution skills and model them for your children. If your goal is to return to your relationship when your partner has been successfully treated, you will want to maintain your relationships with support systems and counselors. Family counseling can also be helpful in establishing healthy communication patterns. A partner who has served time in jail but has not entered treatment should receive treatment before entering joint counseling.

A WORD TO ABUSIVE PARTNERS

If you are reading this, and can acknowledge that this section is talking to you, you may already be accepting the seriousness of your violent behavior. As we've said, there is never an excuse for violence against another individual. You have not been domestically violent because of your partner's or children's actions or behavior. You have been violent because you have a need to be in control of, and have power over, your partner, your children or your own vulnerability. You should seek help immediately from a qualified professional who specializes in the treatment of individuals that are domestically violent.

Perhaps you have a substance abuse problem for which you need treatment. If you think you do, submit to an evaluation by an individual who specializes in substance abuse counseling. Keep in mind, however, that drinking and using drugs has not caused you to be abusive to your partner or children, you have. Abusive behavior doesn't magically stop when you are sober and straight. While drugs and alcohol might be only a part of the problem, sobriety and abstinence from any mind- or mood-altering drugs are a necessary part of the solution.

Whether you think that drugs, alcohol or your past have been the causative factors in leading to your abusiveness, the first step in treatment is admitting that you have a problem and accepting accountability for your behavior. A trained professional can help you understand your triggers for violence. The triggers belong to you, nobody else. For instance, you might strike out immediately when you feel powerless because you don't allow yourself to feel vulnerable. A baby's cry may set you off, or your partner saying "no." Part of accepting responsibility is learning to recognize triggers and the build-up of violence. By recognizing the consequences of your behavior and working at control, you will learn to take time out instead of striking out. You might need to leave the house or get out of the car and take a walk. You might seek out a supportive friend who can listen. Qualified individuals can begin to help you develop plans that will allow you to take responsibility for your violent impulses.

Another part of taking responsibility is removing from your possession or easy reach the weapons that you used or considered using in the past, or giving them to someone you trust outside your home. Don't give them to your partner or your child. That's just a potential set-up. Asking someone to keep lethal weapons for you obviously doesn't stop the impulse to hit or stop you from hurting another. Such an action, though, limits access to guns, knives, and so on, which, considering your impulses, should not be around in the first place.

You may need a complete medical workup. Let your doctor know about your violent impulses and behavior. In a very small number of cases, individuals that are violent have a medical problem that is a partial factor in causing it. Be sure to have a copy of your medical evaluation sent to the treatment professional with whom you are working.

If you're a man, your counselor may suggest that you become part of a men's group. For a man, being in a group with other men that are domestically violent can be effective in two ways:

- The hardest person to con is another con. You have been deceiving yourself and others for a long time. Other men who have operated on the same system of denial and rationalization can be effective confronting you on your behavior. If all the members in the group are new, you might join each other in mutual denial and rationalization in the initial phase of the group. If there are members that have been in the group longer, they will most likely call you on your behavior immediately.

- If you are like most men, you probably have few, if any, supportive male friends. When I say supportive, I mean friends with whom you can share feelings and concerns. It is not helpful to reach out to individuals that will share stories of conquest or join you in mutual denial that your partners are the ones with all the problems.

I think men as a whole have gotten the "short end of the stick" in the areas of emotional expression and needs. I have four sons, and I know men have feelings and needs for support just like women. Many of the attitudes that are believed to be "male" are really the effects of the environment that has shaped you. We are carefully taught and socialized differently. The culture as a whole repeatedly teaches men that they shouldn't have feelings and they need to be "tough."

The male models you grew up around probably had few people they could go to for support. If you have a partner who meets all of your emotional needs, such a situation can frequently bring out feelings of dependency that feed into the violence. A group can help you develop other options and choices. Men often seek out women for emotional support, but many men I have talked to say that the best gift they have given themselves is developing quality relationships with other men.

An important part of your healing is to begin to recognize, name and accept your feelings: joy, anger, sadness, fear, shame, pride, vulnerability. . . . Not only does this lead to healthy expression, but it will also allow you to have greater empathy with the victims of your violence. I can feel compassion and empathy for another who is sad or afraid, because I have allowed myself to experience sadness and fear.

The cliché that you can only love when you have self-love is oft-repeated because it's true. Long ago, you protected yourself by exchanging the need for love and nurturing for the need for power and control. As stated by Maria Roy, exploitive power is not really power at all. Rather, it is violence disguised as a form of power, for at its very essence is an extremely small and very frail self-image that is desperately yearning to be recognized, acknowledged and fortified; a self-image so negative that it seeks to destroy itself by destroying others. (1982, p. 4)

Many perpetrators of domestic violence have told me that they stopped feeling. They feel numb inside and isolated. Controlling other people does not fill the empty space. Power feeding on itself is a self-perpetuating and endless, yet emotionally and spiritually empty cycle. It is important to gain access to the feelings hiding behind the need for power and control.

You can't blame your childhood for your violence today. Not everyone who grows up with violence and pain inflicts violence and pain on others. Your behavior is not genetic, it is learned. After you experience your physical birth, it takes eight years of life to achieve emotional birth. Your adult caretakers are your models. You learn about yourself and how to behave from them. Unfortunately, the mirrors aren't always clear and you can develop a distorted image of yourself as well as behaviors that hurt you and others. Part of your treatment will be learning new communication skills that you didn't learn in the past as well as reclaiming feelings you may have detached long ago.

A FEW WORDS ABOUT DENIAL TO CARE PROVIDERS

I am surprised by the number of the people in the mental health field that tell me they would never treat an abusive partner, a rapist or a person that would abuse a child. If we asked all U.S. and Canadian victims of domestic violence and rape to go to their capitol buildings in Washington, D.C., and Ottawa, there would not be enough room in the capital cities to hold all of us. Every victim has a perpetrator. Mental heath practitioners who pretend that these individuals don't exist are in a tragic form of denial. Yet based on the number of treatment programs available for referral, we can assert that many professionals are refusing to deal with these cases or to believe they have perpetrators on their caseloads.

Occasionally when I have been asked to consult on a case, I hear something in the counselor's description of a person's history or behavior that causes me to ask, "Has this person ever been domestically violent? Are you concerned that this individual may be a rapist? Do you think this person may be abusive to children?" I am often told that the counselor has never questioned the potential for violence in a client, even when the therapist clearly fears the individual. We are often in so much denial that we don't pay attention to the warning signals.

Counselors who have been in the field for a while who tell me that they've never seen an abusive partner or a rapist are most likely in denial. One therapist told me that he knew why I had more perpetrators and victims of violence on my caseload than he did, "I realized it's because you ask the questions. I don't because I don't think I have wanted to know the answers."

Sadly, many victims who go to mental health centers, private therapists, alcohol treatment centers, hospitals or doctors' offices with other presenting problems have never been asked if they have been raped or if they are currently, or ever had been, physically abused by a partner, an adult child or someone else close to them. One woman told me that she had seen a physician and a counselor continually during the seven years she had been abused by her partner, yet she had never talked about it. "I was ashamed to tell them and they never asked. I guess I did a good job of hiding the bruises."

Cooperation Among Mental Health Professionals

Physicians, nurses, alcohol treatment counselors, psychologists, social workers, family therapists, school counselors, safe-home personnel, child care workers, home health personnel, hospice volunteers and other health providers should all be cross-trained in the areas of domestic violence and sexual assault by people who are knowledgeable in each area. Service providers should be aware of local specialists who can provide ongoing or case-specific consultation. All of these professionals need to be aware of what each other can do to form a team to help the suffering victims of abuse, recognize perpetrators of abuse and, at the very least, refer them to professionals who can competently treat them. If treatment programs are not available in your area, advocate for them.

Effective teamwork is not only wise, but necessary. Besides the medical and psychological professionals, advocate groups, crisis workers, support workers, victim support groups and members of the criminal justice system are available to work with victims and perpetrators of violence and sexual assault as well as their families. When multiple care providers and advocates are working together for an individual, working as a team is in the best interest of the individual and the continued safety of the potential victims and society. If an abusive partner or rapist is on probation, the probation officer should be part of the team. Many times lethal individuals slip through the cracks because we don't work together. Many violent individuals actively work to split the system, knowing that their continued freedom depends on our inability to communicate or work effectively as a team.

Care providers frequently develop tunnel vision, remaining so focused on one piece of the puzzle that the larger picture is never seen. Individuals with whom we work depend on our ability to work together and cooperate with one another. One victim of domestic violence talked to me about the time when so many professionals and advocates were giving her different advice that she felt at times that she had to choose a side. "I was already dealing with violence in my marriage. I sure didn't need my 'helpers' at odds. It seemed that everyone I was working with had a totally different notion of what 'was best for me.' Don't you guys ever talk to each other?"

THE IMPORTANCE OF SKILLED SCREENING

Every community needs well-trained professionals that are skilled in the assessment and treatment of abusive partners and rapists. Not all rapists are the same, nor are all abusive partners the same. Although some people would not agree with me, I believe many perpetrators can be treated while others are incurably lethal and not treatable.

Perpetrators that are treatable need to be held accountable for their behavior. Serving time in jails and prisons, however, is not enough. They also need a step-by-step, multifaceted treatment approach.

Through my work in communities, I talk to family and extended family members of individuals that are physically or sexually abusive. Many tell me that they are prevented from reporting abuse because of both concern and fear of reprisal. A large number have said that they would have reported their relative immediately if they knew that treatment would accompany jail time.

I ask these individuals what they would do if they knew in advance that a competent assessment would be completed as a first step in the process. I let them know that the assessment results might reveal that their relatives may not be treatable and that jail could be the only option that would continue to provide safety for the family and community. I was surprised by their answers. They indicated that they would report them anyway if they knew the assessment would be conducted by a fair and competent professional and that their safety would be ensured. As one sister said, "At least I would know. I wouldn't wonder if he could be helped or not. I wouldn't feel as guilty for reporting him."

Most community members have said they wished they had more knowledge about perpetrators of domestic violence and rape. "Our community is full of perpetrators. Why do we always play 'I've Got a Secret' with this issue? Care providers are as guilty of this as anyone else. The media terrifies us and glorifies violence.

Who's going to educate us about it and dispel the myths?"

In some communities I've worked in, adults bring their children to presentations on domestic violence. After these presentations, children as young as five have asked me if I would please help their moms and dads. They usually end with, "I really love them, but I don't like the fights." Children seem to remember what adults have forgotten.

Families and communities deserve to be protected from those individuals that commit violent acts on others. If we are going to stop domestic violence and rape, we must also have in every community skilled professionals that can provide treatment for victims and families. We must also have treatment for those perpetrators who are motivated and treatable. Skilled assessment is essential in order to support families and keep them safe.

Three books that I would recommend for individuals wanting to know more about perpetrators are: *Men Who Rape: The Psychology of the Offender* by A. Nicholas Groth with H. Jean Birnbaum; *The Abusive Partner: An Analysis of Domestic Battering,* edited by Maria Roy; and *When Men Batter Women: New Insights into Ending Abusive Relationships* by Neil Jacobson and John Gottman. Other useful books are available as well. Ask advocates, counselors or other health providers for additional references.

RAPE

The Rape of Women

According to Department of Justice statistics, there are 500,000 sexual assaults on women in the United States annually, including

170,000 rapes and 140,000 attempted rapes. A 1993 Crime Victimization survey reported much higher numbers. According to that survey, 700,000 sexual assaults annually take place on women in the United States. Even with that higher number, most officials believe that the majority of rapes and attempted rapes are still not reported. Victims feel shame and fear, and continue to believe that the rape is their fault. Many women also fear reprisals from their partners or other family members. A surprising portion of society still blames the victim.

Years ago I worked for a time as a rape crisis worker. One night I talked with a young woman at a local hospital who had just been gang-raped. Four young men followed her home. She was carrying a bag of groceries and left her door open for a split second. The men entered her apartment. They beat her, threw her against her kitchen table and took turns raping her. She was brutally assaulted by four men, yet her boyfriend left her and her father screamed at her that she was "no daughter of his." Even her mother felt that she wouldn't have been followed home and assaulted if she hadn't been wearing "such a short skirt."

Many people in our society today still believe that rape is the woman's fault because of the way she dresses, or behaves, or because she was drinking, or perhaps even because she knew the man who raped her. People who believe this myth also usually believe that men can't control their sexual urges, that men have runaway hormones and can't be expected to regain control after they have been sexually aroused. Of course neither of these myths is true, any more than the myth that rape is about sex.

Like other forms of violence, rape is a means of using domination, control and being in charge to discharge resentment, frustration and rage. It is not about sex. As stated so well by Thoko Matshe in *The Myths of Rape* (1997), "Rape is not sex! Rape is violence. If I hit you on the head with a rolling pin you won't call it cooking."

The National Institute of Mental Health conducted a study during 1984 and 1985 and found that one out of nine college women reported being raped. Eight out of ten knew their attacker. One in twelve college men admitted committing acts that met the legal definition of rape or attempted rape, yet only about 1 percent of those that responded felt that their behavior was criminal. In most cases, date rape is justified by the rapist: "She wanted sex. . . . She participated. . . . She was just drunk and doesn't remember she wanted it too." When a woman is drunk or passed out, she obviously can't give informed consent. Sex without consent is rape. While in the act of planning or commiting a rape, the consequences of the behavior have no meaning to the rapist. The only thing that matters is power and control.

Bill was twenty-one when I met him. He had raped a woman in college when he was nineteen. He had served no jail time and was instead put on probation and required to attend a sexual assault group. When I first saw Bill, he had just finished college. He and the woman with whom he was living had come in for couples counseling. After the initial interview, however, I believed that Bill needed individual counseling. I also referred him to a local men's group run by a counselor who had committed sexual offenses in his early years. The counselor now ran groups for young men that had been convicted of date rape, and the focus of the groups was personal accountability.

Bill's responses to my questions in the initial interview led me to believe that he was still in denial regarding the seriousness of his assaultive behavior. He implied that the charges against him really weren't that serious. "I was a young college kid sowing my oats. I know I shouldn't have done it, but the girl was attracted to me too. She gave me a lot of clues that she wanted us to have sex. It wasn't just me, but I guess the guy's always responsible, right?"

The young woman in question was eighteen. She had shared a history class with Bill. They shared a common interest in the Civil War period and had studied together on a number of occasions. Bill had invited her to a fraternity party. They both had been drinking. After the party, he invited her to his room "to talk." Once in the room, Bill became sexually aggressive. She rejected his advances, telling him that she was not ready for a sexual relationship. He accused her of playing "hard to get." He eventually raped her. He took her home and before leaving asked her if she would like to have coffee before class the next morning.

The young woman didn't report the rape, feeling it was her fault because she had been drinking and she didn't want her parents to know. Her roommate, who had also been a victim of date rape, convinced her to call the police.

Bill had been raised in a family with an emotionally abusive father. His mother had been ill from the time Bill was two and had died of cancer when he was four. His father was the primary caretaker and had never remarried. He was, in Bill's words, "a womanizer."

Bill's father frequently called him a "sissy" and always pressured Bill to excel in sports. Even when he was in elementary school, he was pushed to "be the best." When Bill didn't score a goal, his father told him that he was ashamed of him and that "he was no son of his." He told Bill that one way or another he was "going to make him a man."

Bill's father also "educated" him about sex at an early age, telling him that "when women say no they really mean yes." As long as Bill could remember, his father also shared stories of his own sexual "conquests."

When Bill was seven, he had been fondled by an older boy at camp. "I obviously couldn't tell my dad, he already thought I was a 'sissy.' I've never told anyone." Bill also admitted that he didn't like sports and would much rather have spent his time drawing, "Boy, I really wasn't the man my dad wanted. I guess I failed him."

When working with people like Bill, therapists need to be highly confrontative about accountability for their adult actions, originally focusing on denial and lack of empathy for the victim far more than childhood issues, which cannot be used as an excuse for adult actions. As in working with abusive partners, treatment is only effective when the adult individual is consistently held accountable, while the person giving treatment shows compassion for the injured child within. As long as we continue to rationalize the behavior of sexually assaultive individuals and blame victims, rapes will continue to be endured in silence.

In many communities gang rape has increased at an alarming rate. One young woman told me that gang rape had been occurring in her community for as long as anyone can remember. "It has become so common that in this community it is almost viewed as a girl's 'rite of passage' into womanhood. We are suppose to take it and shut up. When I was sixteen I finally worked up the courage to tell my aunt that I had been raped by five men when I first turned fifteen. She told me that it happened to her, too, and that I should just forget about it and not say anything."

Even though it has achieved very little attention, the mass rape of women has happened repeatedly in time of war. The February 22, 1993, issue of *Time* magazine reported the following statistics: The Japanese people raped and sometimes murdered thousands of Chinese women in Nanjing in 1937. Soviet soldiers "paid back" the Nazis by raping 2 million German women in 1945. Pakistani troops raped more than 250,000 Bengali women and girls in Bangladesh in 1971. In 1993, a European Community team of investigators calculated that 20,000 Muslim women and girls had been raped in Bosnia since the war began. The Bosnian government reported that as many as 50,000 rapes had already occurred. And the list goes on. (Morrow, 1993)

From the endless statistics, we see that rape is clearly an instrument of war. The killing of soldiers in war lessens the number of fighting men and makes martyrs. The rape of young girls and women deeply injures the spirit of an enemy and, in many cases, the cultural identity and the values of a nation.

The Rape of Men

Although incidents of male rape are few compared to reported rapes by women, most experts believe that men raping men is far more common than is currently believed. I have treated six men that have been raped. Two had referred themselves to treatment because of long-term depression; one because of increased panic attacks and the fourth for substance abuse. All had experienced sexual dysfunction in their relationships and three had never been able to make a commitment to a relationship. Even so, they originally said they had never been raped and only spoke about the episodes after a great deal of trust had been achieved. Two of the six were raped in prison and related the incidents early in their treatment.

Of the four men that were raped outside of an institutional setting, three were raped while hitchhiking and one was raped while hiking alone in a remote area. All of the men had been forced into submission through the use of weapons. All four of the rapists threatened to kill their victims if they wouldn't "cooperate." Three intimidated their victims with knives and the other used a gun.

All four were also forced to achieve ejaculation through stimulation by their captors. This action seemed to cause the most shame because the men believed their sexual response implied consent. As one man told me, "How could I have responded sexually to him?" All of the men felt lesser as men because they "allowed" themselves to be raped. Their intense shame caused them to keep the rapes a secret for years. In all four cases, I was the first person they had told, and I believe it was only because I asked.

As is the case with sexual assault against women, the rape of men has little to do with sex and far more to do with power, control and sexualized aggression. Rape in prison—which is reported with more regularity—frequently involves status-seeking, power and superiority within the institutional setting. One man told me that his attacker was serving a sentence for repeated sexual assaults on women. The other man in my care was gang-raped by four prison inmates who told him that it was part of his initiation into prison life. He told me the initiation period never ended.

According to A. Nicholas Groth in *Men Who Rape: The Psychology of the Offender*, it is a myth that only homosexuals commit rapes against men. He stated that to half of the rapists in his study of rapes outside prisons, the gender of the victim had no relevance. The other rapists were homosexual and bisexual. Several of the prison inmates who raped fellow prisoners had prior convictions for sexual assaults against women. Note, however, that his study of male rapes contains a very small number of case studies, and a great deal more research is needed in this area.

A Few Words to the Victims of Rape

Most importantly, rape is not your fault. A rapist is an individual with psychological problems that have nothing to do with you. You are probably not the first victim and probably won't be the last, unless the perpetrator is stopped. Remember, too, that rape is not a sexual act. It is an act fueled by the need for power, control and sexualized aggression.

If you have been raped recently, seek help and protection immediately. If you are not seeking help because of the attitudes of those around you, remember that changing myths is sometimes a long process, but you deserve to start your own recovery process and there are many who have shared your pain and many others who can validate your feelings. Remember you are one of millions that have been raped, and resources are available to help you. Seek out a counselor at the rape crisis center in your community or a community nearby. This individual can validate your experience and provide a much-needed buffer from further shaming at a time when you are the most vulnerable. The counselor may also help you get through a difficult legal process.

If you were raped in the past, and are still experiencing post-traumatic effects—night terrors, panic attacks, anxiety, flashbacks, difficulty in relationships, depression, rage, sexual dysfunction, hypervigilance, fear of the ordinary, shame—seek counseling or a victim support group. Remember, you are having symptoms of post-traumatic stress, a normal response to an abnormal and painful act. Many trauma survivors confuse the abnormality of the trauma with abnormality of the self.

If you are in a relationship, your counselor might suggest that your partner or other family members attend a support group as well. If there is not a support group in your area for the relatives and partners of rape victims, you might suggest that your significant other talk to a counselor at the rape crisis clinic or another knowledgeable professional. If your family receives support and education, they might be able to better support you in your process of recovery.

Rape victims often tell me that they have gone through many stages in their recovery. One woman put it this way: "First I thought there was something wrong with me. With the help of advocacy and counseling, I was able to see myself as a victim who was not responsible for the rape. As time passed, I was able to see myself as a survivor and appreciate the strength of a woman who survived a horrendous trauma. Now, I see myself as a human being who has experienced the painful effects of senseless violence."

A Word to Rapists or Those Concerned That They Might Commit Rape

If you have committed rape or are concerned that you might, or if you committed sexual assault years ago and have never been treated, get help immediately. Rape is both compulsive and violent. It is fueled by the need for power and control, as well as by aggression that has become sexualized. Sometimes, but not always, rapists have had early compulsive behaviors prior to their first rape that steadily increased over time. These compulsive behaviors may have been fire setting, voyeurism, obscene phone calls, interest in violent pornography, exposing oneself, increasing fantasies of committing rapes, fantasizing about particular victims or stalking.

You may also believe that people really want to have sex with you and mean "yes" when they say "no," or perhaps you are increasingly aggressive with the objects of your affection (rough fondling or kissing that is aggressive). If you have these behaviors, seek professional help. The first step is to recognize that you have a problem that requires treatment.

Some men that have been concerned about compulsive behaviors and their potentially lethal nature have voluntarily requested assessment and treatment. Many men who have participated in gang rapes as teenagers have been concerned enough about their past behavior to refer themselves for assessment and treatment. More and more college students that are concerned that their attitudes about women might lead to date rape are seeking help.

If you are concerned about yourself, a friend or a family member, please seek professional help.

A COMMUNITY APPROACH TO DOMESTIC VIOLENCE AND SEXUAL ASSAULT

In order to begin to arrest the national epidemic of domestic violence and sexual assaults, communities must develop zero-tolerance policies. To some extent, domestic violence has continued over the years because community members tolerate it, deny it or ignore it. Rapists and perpetrators of other sexual assaults aren't held accountable and treated because of the unspoken norm of silence and the tendency to blame the victim. When we don't act, we give silent approval to violent behavior. There should never be a reason to witness violence without intervening: offering assistance, getting help or, at the very least, calling the police.

I promised myself years ago that I would no longer participate in child abuse by being another set of adult eyes watching and doing nothing. Often I offer the parent assistance and then sit down and talk about the abuse. A tragedy in itself is the shock and surprise often registered that anyone would actually offer assistance. After the initial shock and accompanying defense, the assistance is, in many cases, gratefully accepted. Many people have written to me, letting me know that they have followed up on the referrals I offered. Others that I have talked to have also tried compassionate intervention in situations that are not dangerous with the same result.

When it seems too dangerous to intervene, I call for assistance. For instance, I once heard a man yelling at his child. As I approached, I saw that he had tied his child to a tree and was screaming at her while threatening her with a belt. I sensed that the situation was dangerous and that he wasn't approachable. I immediately called the police, then Child Protective Services. I later found out that the little girl had heroically tried to stop her father from continuing to beat her mother and was threatened and tied to a tree for her effort.

Stopping violence is a community effort, and many people have begun to take action. In one community, for instance, a group of men assertively and compassionately confront men that are domestically violent. They offer support while at the same time letting the individual know that violence against women and children will not be tolerated. Some of the men taking part in the interventions have been abusive partners in the past and through a great deal of personal work have become powerful voices against violence to women and children. This community also has a volunteer hot line staffed by men who abusive partners can call before striking out. Temporary housing provisions are offered for a much-needed "time out." One thing that has struck me in working with abusive partners is their degree of isolation. Many have no support systems and have been raised by fathers that had few friends.

This type of community action from men can begin to change community norms while, at the same time, offering a different model for boys and men. Men are violent when they feel that it is permissible to dominate others and to use force to resolve problems. When peer-group pressure supports equality and compassion rather than violence, much-needed changes will occur.

In most communities there are advocates for women and children suffering from domestic violence as well as safe homes and emergency hot lines. Even with these resources, some women have a great deal of difficulty reaching out, have been abandoned by friends, are unsupported by family or have been forced into isolation by abusive partners. These women, as well as home-bound elderly, may need to have others reach out to them. One woman said that she would never have called an advocate or the emergency hot line if it had not been for a supportive neighbor that "didn't give up on me." She had gone to a therapist at one time who told her that she would not see her if she wouldn't leave her husband.

Other communities have drop-in centers for parents who are concerned that they might harm a child. These centers are, for the most part, staffed by older adults that have been effective parents and can listen and provide support as well as advice and referral when necessary. Well-screened volunteers provide child care, allowing the parents to have temporary "time out."

Many colleges are also developing zero tolerance for date rape and are letting students know when they are admitted the seri-ousness of the issue on that campus and that sexual assault is not only a criminal offense, but is an act that injures the entire college community and will result in expulsion.

A large number of colleges are requiring date-rape seminars as a part of their orientation. Female students are advised to stay together at parties and watch out for one another.

In some college communities, compassionate male students who are angered by the increasing incidents of sexual assault to women have formed groups that provide escort services to and from classes in the evening. They provide a type of escort service to parties when requested. These young men don't drink in order to watch out for women students who have requested their help because they have decided to drink at a particular party.

Some young men have begun to confront fellow male students on previously accepted though inappropriate behavior, including stories of "conquest," or comments that are insulting to women. One young man told me, "It would be far more difficult if I was the only person trying to make a difference, but many of us who have always objected to emotional and physical violence towards women are waking up and standing together. I think a lot of men have always been disgusted by 'sexist' behavior, but have remained silent because of peer pressure. If we stand together, we can create a different kind of peer pressure."

In other communities, women have formed "We Care" task forces, encouraging young women to break the silence: "We are here to listen to them, support them and validate their experiences. People have been silent in this community too long."

Some women who live in a community where gang rape had been epidemic displayed pictures of their young women/victims in the Community Center. Under the pictures were stories personalizing each girl, telling others who they were and who their relatives were. A big banner above said, "Help Us Watch Out for Our Daughters, Granddaughters, Nieces and Sisters. Help Us Keep Them Safe." As community awareness increased and people began watching out for their youth, the incidents of gang rape decreased. Because of the validation of a group of community women, young women have begun to feel supported enough to break the silence.

All communities can develop creative solutions like these to the epidemic of domestic violence and sexual assault, but individuals must first open their eyes and ears to the problem. Communities must develop zero tolerance for violence and adopt norms and values that are modeled by adults and passed on to future generations.

I was reminded of the compassion that exists in my rural Vermont community when a neighbor that lives some distance away called late one night. She wanted to let me know that a delivery man had stopped by her house asking for my address. She said the man appeared to be drinking and she was concerned. She knew that I had recently been widowed and wanted to alert me that the man was on his way. Her call let me know that she was watching out for me. In this time of abundance, perhaps the greatest gift available is the compassion that one community member can give to another.

"I'm Not Angry, but I've Got a Lot of Killing to Do"

"The web we weave is increasingly toxic, hostile to the human spirit. Our actions form the walls of our prisons."

—SHARIF M. ABDULLAH

Fifteen-year-old Kip had warned students at his school that "something bad was going to happen." Friends of the family said he had become increasingly difficult for his parents to discipline and had developed a fascination with guns, knives and bombs. A friend said that he had downloaded instructions on bomb-making from the Internet.

Kip's parents had allegedly sent him to anger-management classes, which Kip had convinced them he no longer needed. His father had reportedly bought him a 9mm Glock semiautomatic pistol and a .22 caliber semiautomatic rifle, thinking that he could redirect his son's fascination with bombs and guns into a supervised hobby.

Then on May 20, 1998, he was expelled from school and arrested for bringing a pistol to school. He was later released in the custody of his parents. Shortly after returning home, he reportedly shot his father in the head. Later that day when his mother came home from work, he killed her.

He presumably stayed with his parents' bodies all night. At 7:30 the next morning, dressed in a dark trenchcoat, he drove his family's van to the school that had previously expelled him. At about 7:55 he entered the school through a side door in the cafeteria where approximately three hundred students were gathered. He pulled out a .22 caliber semiautomatic rifle and opened fire on his classmates. He then slowed down a bit and walked across the room, taking aim at students and shooting some at point-blank range. When he ran out of the fifty rounds of ammunition held by the .22 and began to reload, a fellow student that had been wounded in the stomach tackled Kip from behind. Others came to assist. Students would later say that Kip was incredibly calm the entire time he was shooting and that he had a "normal" look on his face.

In the last several years, children as young as six have been charged with sexual assault, murder or both. Four boys in

Cincinnati were recently charged with the sexual assault of a seven-year-old girl. The boys ranged in age between eight and ten.

In the nine months between October 1997 and June 1998, fifteen people were killed and forty-two were wounded in multiple-victim school shootings in the United States. The shock for many was that these shootings didn't take place in huge metropolitan cities like New York, Detroit or Los Angeles. Instead, students opened fire in much smaller areas: Pearl, Mississippi; West Paducah, Kentucky; Stamps, Arkansas; Jonesboro, Arkansas. The youths that committed these senseless shootings ranged in age from eleven to seventeen. They weren't gang members or delinquents. For the most part, these kids had good grades and no criminal records.

In each case, though, many community members knew the youths were troubled but didn't believe that the end results would be murder, even when the boys warned others of their intentions. One woman questioned, "What in the world is happening to our kids? Why are they doing these senseless attacks on their fellow classmates and teachers?" Another asked, "Where are the adults?" These are very good questions. Hundreds might ask, "What is happening?" but a more pressing question might be, "What are we going to do about it?"

Concerns about youth aren't new, but today's types of concern are different. Many parents are telling me that part of their elementary schoolchild's language includes threats of violence: "I'm going to kill you." "I'm going to shoot you." "I wish you would die." These statements are not reserved for peers, but said to parents as well.

Elementary school teachers are shocked when children ask

them to "make love." Children have far more information than they can developmentally handle.

Kids these days have proven themselves capable of gruesome acts of violence, senseless killings that involve sexual acting out and mass murder. Our children are giving us a wake-up call, but to what?

One concern should be popular culture. Many things are happening in the media that might explain some of the increase in violence among our youth. Our children are systematically becoming desensitized to violence through television, videos, music and movies. Video games are using the same techniques of operant conditioning that were used to train soldiers in Vietnam. Young people have easy access to weapons.

At home, the family unit is breaking down. As a result, children are seeking role models outside the home, often on television and in the movies where positive models are sometimes hard to locate. Family violence is epidemic. Values that support concern for one another are disappearing. Society is adopting values that encourage violence.

In this book we have already discussed in a general fashion many of these concerns. Let's now take a closer look.

DESENSITIZATION AND OPERANT CONDITIONING

Books and movies about the heroic actions of our soldiers in World War I and World War II are commonplace. What is rarely mentioned is that during these wars, only 15 to 20 percent of combat veterans were willing to fire a shot at another human being (Grossman, 1995). According to researchers, reluctance to shoot another had nothing to do with fear. Soldiers showed tremendous bravery. Instead, the unwillingness to fire a shot at another human being demonstrated the individual's natural aversion to killing.

In his book *On Killing: The Psychological Cost of Learning to Kill in War and Society* (1995, pp. 3–4, 30, 35), Lt. Col. David Grossman presents the results of research conducted by G. Dyer, R. Gabriel and S. L. A. Marshall asserting that the vast majority of soldiers in both world wars never fired a shot. Most fighter pilots, furthermore, never shot anyone down or even tried to. Grossman contends that even though many people ignored the research of individuals like Marshall, the U.S. Army did not. They changed training procedures for the military, with the result that 55 percent of soldiers in Korea fired their weapons. Still other advanced techniques spurred by greater developments in technology and psychology resulted in 90 to 95 percent of our soldiers being willing to kill in Vietnam. The techniques that were so successful in training the military in Vietnam—progressive desensitization and operant conditioning—are now increasingly offered to the general population. Desensitization techniques used to train military personnel in Vietnam involved increasing exposure to films that showed explicit and brutal footage of people being violently injured and killed. The senseless and brutal violence shown to soldiers in the military to teach them to kill is frighteningly similar to the visuals currently available to our youth in movie theaters, on television and in video games.

As Grossman stated, adolescents—in movie theaters across the nation and in front of the television at home—are seeing details of horrible suffering and killing of human beings, and they are learning to associate this killing and suffering with entertainment, pleasure, their favorite soft drink, their favorite candy bar and the close intimate contact of their date.

When one of my sons was six or seven, a teacher in school showed the movie *Hiroshima*. My son was frightened for weeks, worrying that "everyone was going to be killed." He had trouble sleeping and had nightmares most nights. This teacher, in his wish to show young children the graphic pain inflicted on others in war, forgot that these children were developmentally incapable of processing the information.

I spent many nights with my son trying to help him process his feelings and understand this information. I wondered how many parents did. How many were aware of the effects of violent films on children? When children are surrounded by or shown violence, they become anxious and afraid. If this fear is not worked through and the stimulus continues, they survive through numbing. This is the process of becoming desensitized to violence.

A tremendous number of children in the United States today are assuredly unable to process the violence that they see on television, in the news and in videos. We are raising children who, like the soldiers in Vietnam, are becoming desensitized to violence. They see movies like *Reservoir Dogs, Casino, Goodfellas, Independence Day, Menace to Society* and TV shows like *Jerry Springer* and *South Park*. Children and youth are watching PG-13 and R-rated movies on cable TV and in-home videos. Children who feel neglected, unpopular or bullied often spend a great deal of time unsupervised watching television and videos that have not been first screened by an adult close to them who cares.

As the desensitization process continues, children crave more and more stimulus. A few years ago, junior-high-age kids were stimulated by watching movies with realistic deaths. One popular series was *Faces of Death*, which featured footage of people actually dying. Personally, I covered my eyes and turned my head watching the original *Psycho*—a movie thought to be incredibly violent for its time—but the visual impact of the violence in that movie is attributable mostly to the skill of the director and film editor. Today's movies, which make *Psycho* look like *The Sound of Music*, use special effects and an unblinking camera eye to record the details of violent acts from start to finish. Kids watch realistic, graphic death scenes and unspeakable acts of violence and don't even flinch.

B. F. Skinner believed that a child's mind was a blank slate and that the children could be turned into anything if their environment could be controlled at a young age. Unlike earlier theories of personality development, Skinner, in his theory of operant conditioning, promulgated the belief that all behavior is a result of reward and punishment. The U.S. Armed Forces used Skinner's theory in order to create a highly effective fighting force in Vietnam, a force whose soldiers shot 90 to 95 percent of the time, unlike the soldiers in World War I and II. Unfortunately, American society is creating violent youth using the same operant conditioning methods.

- An adolescent stands in front of a firing range. A silhouette shaped like a man pops up in front of him. He fires. The man falls down. Then another man and another. Two more fall down. This soldier in the making has received positive reinforcement each time a man falls. The adolescent has earned many marksmanship medals. He won't have to think twice about killing a man. Earlier in his life he was desensitized to violence. Now he had been conditioned to kill upon command.

- An eight-year-old stands mesmerized in front of a screen. A voice in the background cries "Help me! Help me!" His eyes are fixed on the screen in front of him, gun in hand ready to shoot. An image of a man in a dark suit pops up, and the child fires. A direct hit! The man lurches and falls over backwards, a red mark on his head where the bullet entered. Another pops up. . . . The child fires again. The figure grabs at the red area on his arm. The boy shoots once more, this time a direct hit. Three more arise, now the child turns to reload. Another pops up. For his age, the child exhibits lightning-fast reflexes and judgment with a trigger. Don't shoot, it is not a man in a dark suit. He fires again at a different figure. Another fatal hit. The figure lurches back and falls over. It has been a good day. The shooting has been accurate. The child has been rewarded each time a man falls. Now comes the reward of a high score. He is proud of his accuracy. This boy is not being trained to kill on demand. He is not a soldier. He is just being trained to kill.

- A seven-year-old who had been playing a video game for hours was asked by his aunt, "Why is it so important for you to keep getting to a different level?" The child, still intent on his game, answered, "Because if you don't get to the next level, either the police will arrest you or the bad guys will kill you. You have to kill them first."

Grossman comments, "If we had a clear-cut objective of raising a generation of assassins and killers who are unrestrained by either authority or the nature of the victim, it is difficult to imagine how we could do a better job." (1995, p. 310)

A NATION OF WEAPONS

A thirteen-year-old and an eleven-year-old opened fire on their schoolmates in Jonesboro, Arkansas, a town of fifty-one thousand in the northeast corner of the state. This thirteen-year-old drove his parents' van to a secluded area behind Westside Middle School. The van contained "survival gear" and large quantities of ammunition. The boys had seven handguns and two high-powered rifles. They were dressed in camouflage and found a good spot that was protected by some trees, yet still allowed a clear view of the schoolyard. The boys put in their earplugs. One of the boys pulled the school's fire alarm box, forcing the students and teachers out of the building and into their line of fire. They then opened fire, scoring fifteen hits in less than a minute, killing four students and a teacher who used her body to protect a student.

Magazine covers showcased the eleven-year-old as a smiling toddler dressed in camouflage and holding a rifle. Other articles showed the same child at six, again dressed in camouflage looking down the barrel of a pistol. Santa had brought him a shotgun when he was six years old. He had worked to improve his aim over the years playing video games at an arcade.

Why are we so obsessed with guns in America? Why would we need a gun at any time that shot fifty rounds of ammunition without needing to be reloaded? I don't believe we have created them to hunt fast-moving rabbits. These guns are for exclusive use on animals of the two-legged variety.

In 1997, guns were the third-leading cause of death of young people between the ages of thirteen and twenty-four. Interestingly enough, in that same year, the House of Representatives passed legislation allowing offenders as young as thirteen to be tried as adults in federal court. I believe wholeheartedly in accountability, yet the logic of this action escaped me. How young will we go? We now have a seven-year-old and eight-year-old arrested for murder. Shall we pass legislation to try them as adults?

There were certainly problems in families when I was growing up. My parents' generation had difficulties, as has every generation. We had domestic violence and child abuse. We had gangs, drugs and alcohol. We didn't, however, have popular athletes sexually assaulting intellectually challenged schoolmates with broomsticks and baseball bats. We didn't have young adolescents killing and mutilating eight-year-old children while practicing a cult ritual. We didn't have children plotting premeditated acts of mass murder.

The youth committing murders are children, chronologically, emotionally and physically. But we are not paying attention to the voices that are literally blasting through our silence. Our prisons are full. How many are we going to build before we realize that what we've been doing is not working? Many ask, where has the innocence of our children gone? I believe it has walked away hand in hand with our adulthood and the accompanying responsibilities. Eleven-year-olds and fourteen-year-olds are in the possession of high-powered rifles. It's not just in Jonesboro, Arkansas, or Springfield, Oregon, or Moses Lake, Washington. It's happening nationwide. What is cute about a toddler dressed in camouflage holding a rifle? How many houses does Santa come to bringing guns? Giving a child access to a gun is like asking the child to drive a Cadillac with a kiddy car steering wheel. Our response is to pay attention to their actions only after they end up in a ditch. And do we even then pay attention to our own actions?

THE BREAKDOWN IN THE FAMILY

It is not surprising in today's world that more children are watching hours of unsupervised television and playing endless hours of video games. Before World War II, at least one grandparent was a full-time active part of most households. Today fewer than 5 percent of our families have a grandparent available as a support and resource. Families lack connection with aunts, uncles, and other extended family. A child at one time had many options for support, encouragement and modeling. Young parents were supported in parenting, one of the most important jobs we will ever do. If a young mother couldn't take care of a child right away, others would.

In approximately fifty years we have gone from a society with the support of an extended family network to a society where communication and support from extended family is the exception. In this new society, families are long distances away, physically and often emotionally as well. Young adults are lacking in needed support in raising young families, while children miss out on the opportunity to learn from and communicate with a variety of adult support systems.

Today's economic conditions are such that both parents often have to work to make ends meet. Coupled with the breakdown of extended family and community networks, these circumstances create far too many latchkey kids—children who come home from school and let themselves into an empty house.

Thousands of parents work out healthy plans for child care and spend quality time with children. Far too many children, however, experience minimal relationships with parents who are too tired, too drunk or loaded, too emotionally drained to communicate much more than rules and demands.

While working with communities throughout the United States and Canada, I frequently ask children and young adults, "If you could have one thing that would make your life better, what would it be?" Ninety percent of the time I hear the following responses: "I want my parents to show an interest in who I am and what I do." "I want more time with my parents." "I want to know that the adults in my life are interested in what I think and feel." "I want to understand my culture and traditions." "I want to feel I belong."

When children do not feel a sense of importance and connection they turn to peers, television and movie heroes or anti-heroes for values and belonging. In far too many cases, we have children influencing and guiding children, and anti-heroes teaching values. Too many adults say, "I'll spend time with you tomorrow," and tomorrow never comes.

Richard Louv, in his disquieting book *Childhood's Future*, speaks about the supportive network that every child needs in order to grow into a healthy adult. He calls this network a web. "The web is emotional as well as physical. As a boy growing up in a troubled family, I sensed that I could get much of what I needed from the web—neighbors to watch out for me on the street, schools that cared, and an understandable community in which to prove myself. . . . Once the web begins to unravel, the smallest bodies fall through first. This is what is happening today." (1990, p. 6)

The type of personality disorders that have their origins in early detachment, such as psychopathy—a disorder where a child does not develop the ability to have empathy and does not have a conscience—rarely, if ever, develops in children who have a web. Society pays an enormous price for children without healthy parenting or other adult suport systems.

A large number of children today feel detached, isolated and disconnected. Many are surrounded by busy, fast-moving adults who feel overwhelmed and frustrated. Children who fail to receive sufficient love from others fail to build a reservoir of self-love or a capacity for self-love. Without this reserve they are unable to deal with the inevitable rejections and humiliations that everyone faces from time to time. They begin to feel numb and dead inside. Many feel an internal contempt for themselves that is disguised under bravado and a need for control and power. They don't express healthy anger. Too frequently they explode, taking years of rage out on family members or society. Some commit suicide, turning years of pent-up rage on themselves.

Let's return to the thirteen-year-old in Jonesboro, Arkansas, who, with his eleven-year-old accomplice, opened fire on his classmates at Westside Middle School. A friend of this young man said that he once became so upset about a breakup with a girl-friend that he threatened suicide. He reportedly showed his friend the rope and gun that he was going to use to end his life. His friend managed to talk him out of it.

The violence that this teenager directed at his fellow students in middle school was reportedly over another romantic disappoint-ment. Some say that he threatened to kill the young woman who would not return his affection. All young teenagers feel rejected at one time or another. Why did the slights from young women in his life lead this young man to the wish to destroy self and others?

According to an article in the April 6, 1998, edition of *Newsweek*, this boy spent his younger years growing up in small towns in Minnesota. Like his eleven-year-old partner in the shootings, he had grown up with guns in the house. A former police chief in one of the small towns in which he had lived reported that he was a "troubled child." The police chief report-edly said that his parents occasionally lost track of him and called the police. He commented that the young boy of eight or nine would sometimes stop by the former chief's house and ask to play with his kids. According to the article, the chief said he "wouldn't allow it."

From the description, it sounds like this boy frequently felt lost. He was from a broken home and his mother worked many hours away in order to make ends meet. She was also reportedly ill for a long period of time. When he lived in Minnesota he was said to have spent a lot of time with his grandmother. He reportedly missed her when he had to move.

The alleged statement from the former small-town police chief bothered me. According to the story, this was a wounded, hurt and sometimes literally "lost" boy of eight or nine. Why wouldn't you invite a child in and offer him support instead of excluding him? Perhaps inclusion in a family would have provided a sense of belonging. Maybe a healthy adult male model could have been crucial at that time, allowing the young boy other choices and options. I believe that community members often underestimate the powerful effect their caring can make in the lives of children.

Children who lack consistent models frequently search for them in the extended family or broader community: a teacher, policeman, spiritual leader, etc. If they don't find them at home or in the community, or new models abuse them as well, they find them instead in rock stars or Hollywood anti-heroes. These unhealthy models are having increasing influence on the lives of our young people.

Unlike the television and movie heroes of my time, today's anti-heroes do not teach healthy values. They teach senseless violence and perform in dramas where you can no longer tell the good guys from the bad guys. Some youth follow models that glorify drugs and violence, like Kurt Cobain (who committed suicide a few years ago), the Ghetto Boys or Snoop Doggy Dog.

Celebrities also provide solace for many adults who aren't connected enough to come to know their next-door neighbor. They focus a tremendous amount of energy, however, keeping up with the lives of actors and actresses, talk show hosts, sports heroes, the Royal Family, and other celebrities. The degree of felt connection and interest shown to these celebrities too frequently is not directed anywhere else. An individual may not sit down for a family dinner, listening to their children share stories of their day and offering their own, but instead relax eating alone while watching sports or a favorite talk show, or pouring over *People* magazine.

We don't seem to have the skill, energy or sometimes the inclination that is required to make personal relationships work. No wonder one out of every two marriages today will end in divorce. We spend hours comparing our lives to those of celebrity models and vicariously find excitement in our own lives through theirs, expecting the same glamour for ourselves.

Many of us feel a sense of isolation and disconnection from those around us. We spend our free time watching television, movies, reading magazines and developing heroes and models far away, or we buy things that only temporarily fill an empty space. It might be very useful for us and for the emotional health of future generations and society to occasionally turn around and look into the faces of the children who are following us.

FAMILY VIOLENCE

Far too many children don't have to turn on their televisions to experience violence. They are surrounded by emotional, physical or sexual violence every day in their homes. Family violence is the chief killer of children under the age of thirteen and of women of all ages. Children under the age of two account for about one-quarter of all child homicides.

Many individuals that work with domestic violence aren't terribly surprised by the senseless killing of children and teachers in our schools at the hands of our youth. Some tell me they are only surprised that it doesn't happen more frequently or that the incidents hadn't begun years earlier.

Perhaps the reason that so many have been shocked by the recent outbreak of child mass murder is that it seems more random and less personal than the man who beats his child to death, or the mother who drowns her children. Maybe it is more shocking because school has been far safer than home for thousands of children. In the past it was far easier for many to deny what was happening behind closed doors. When children begin killing children, it begins to provide us with a societal mirror that has been covered for too long. The problem is no longer theirs, but ours.

Over the years, many people have been shocked when a young person kills a parent. Many ask, "How could they do that?" In the majority of cases, that child or adolescent has been severely beaten, emotionally abused or sexually abused, or all three, for most of their lives. These are not killings of the mercenary type committed by the Menendez brothers. Most incidents of parricide are committed by youth in the defense of their mothers, brothers or sisters. As one young man who had killed his father told me, "I could take it when my dad was beating me, but I couldn't just stand by and witness the brutal beatings of my mother anymore." He also told me that he had learned immediately before the crime that his father had been sexually abusing his sister for years.

When children are constantly exposed to domestic violence, most are first terrified, then enraged, and then, finally, desensitized to violence. The desensitization makes the act of parricide that much "easier."

CHANGING FAMILY VALUES

Rather than learning values that support connectedness and interconnectedness, many children learn values that support violence. As we've mentioned, the long road to emotional birth of a child takes eight years. The child takes from the outside and brings to the inside teachings about self, people and life.

The way a child learns respect is to be respected and to watch adult caretakers treat themselves, others and all of creation with respect. I talked to a parent in a grocery store recently that had just hit her child for hitting his brother. This child is not learning to use words and not strike out, but learns instead that you can hit if you're bigger.

I heard a parent cautioning his child, "You can't let yourself be stepped on. You've got to look out for Number One. If you have to step on a few people on the way, so be it." This lesson from this parent is crystal clear. Another parent might tell a child to care for others and share, and yet cuts in front of everyone in the grocery line. The message that is taught is the one that is seen, not the one that is heard.

I've seen parents teaching their children the benefits of communication and to resolve conflicts in a healthy way, while engaging in a days-long "cold war" with their partner. Again, that which is modeled is learned. Children pay attention to actions far more than words.

The following are nineteen convictions that can lead to competition and violence, rather than connection and cooperation. Check your own way of life against this list, and consider also the actions of society at large:

1) I need it now! Gratification has to happen immediately.

Who wants to save for it? Just buy it on credit.

2) Might is right.

3) Don't get involved.

4) It's important to beat out the other guy, before he gets ahead of you.

5) Get ahead any way you can.

6) Women are objects.

7) Men don't feel.

8) My beliefs are right and yours are wrong.

9) Violence is an appropriate way to handle disagreement.

10) Money is more important than relationships.

11) Talk about people, not to people.

12) I'm not accountable unless I get caught.

13) Blame others for your problems.

14) It's not all right to have emotional needs. Take a pill, be happy.

15) I can only be heard if I talk louder, or show you who's boss.

16) Childhood is overrated. Grow up fast so that I can get on with my life.

17) You can get anything you want if you have enough money.

18) Look out for Number One!

19) Those are your kids, not mine.

POSSIBLE SOLUTIONS

So much is going on in society to contribute to its dissolution that not enough laws could be passed to properly regulate behavior, even assuming that passing laws would be an effective approach or that all manners of behavior should be regulated by elected officials. Nonetheless, some extra controls might assist in needed changes.

First, we need to recognize that children are more important than guns by passing strict gun control laws and laws that advocate elimination of all assault weapons. I doubt seriously that our forefathers had these weapons in mind when they wrote an amendment that guaranteed us the right to bear arms. Parents need to be held accountable for children in the possession of deadly weapons.

We also need tough laws that restrict the glorification of violence and drugs on TV, in movies, in music or on the Internet that could be accessible to children under the age of sixteen. Again, I doubt seriously that our forefathers had this type of material in mind when they wrote an amendment guaranteeing the right of free speech. We often hide behind First Amendment rights.

Society as a whole needs to be educated on the effects of desensitization and operant conditioning. Many parents are not restricting television or video games because they are unaware of these effects. Education will allow them to make informed decisions. One positive though unlikely development would be the restriction of all shows that have violent content, glorify drugs or violence toward women, or use techniques of operant conditioning to children under fourteen. Material on the Internet that teaches the development of any kind of bombs or assault weapons also needs to be restricted.

Day care and elementary school teachers need to be trained to identify children with violence potential, and work with the community to develop prevention programs for these children.

Healthy role models such as Big Brothers, Big Sisters, adopted grandparents, etc., need to be available to these children. These support individuals need to be carefully screened. Young people and their parents should be held accountable for violent or destructive actions toward others.

Grants should be provided for prevention programs for crime, drugs or violence.

All community members should have access to individuals who can teach healthy conflict resolution. Volunteers could be trained to help families work through crisis. I feel that one of the most supportive organizations that exists today is hospice. Hospice volunteers aid families in taking care of people who are dying at home so that individuals can die with dignity. Hospice also supports the family and helps them learn about healthy grieving and connecting with one another. We have families that are literally emotionally dying and need the assistance of healthy, caring community members that are willing to reach out. Many need to be helped to "live" with dignity.

I think it is vital for individuals to become aware of the impact of community disconnection and the breakdown of the extended family. It is sad when individuals feel that they have to legislate values, such as the proposed "good Samaritan" legislation. We seem to have reached a point where we have to "make" parents accountable, technology responsible and community members caring of one another. I think we have reached a "boiling point" where it is necessary for those who are awake to sound the alarm for others, and for us to begin to listen to the warnings of our children. Those that hear need to spread the message.

Hearing from Our Children

"I have heard your words—they have entered one ear and shall not escape the other."

—Sharitarish

We have spoken about the lessons that our children have to teach us through their words and behavior. We have a great deal to learn from them. For this chapter, we asked a group of eight-, nine- and ten-year-olds three questions about violence. Their responses are instructive about how children view the world around them. That children this young are so fluent in the topic of violence in society is a lesson in itself.

EIGHT-YEAR-OLD GIRL:

What is violence?

Violence is something that disturbs the peace in some sort of place.

Why are people violent?

Because they are upset and not mature enough to handle things with words.

What do you think we can do about violence?

First, I think that parents should not yell at their kids or ever get violent with them. They should prevent them from going and doing violent things. Second, I think they should get counseling or professional help.

TEN-YEAR-OLD BOY:

Why is there violence?

Because people are stupid. Cause that's all they know how to do.

Why are people violent?

Because they watch a TV show and they think it's okay.

What do you think we can do about violence?

I think we can help by not doing it.

TEN-YEAR-OLD BOY:

Why is there violence?

Because people are angry at other people. They don't know what to with themselves. They are dared.

Why are people violent?

Because they don't know how to deal with their anger.

What do you think we can do about violence?

We can try and catch the people who are committing these crimes. We should try and teach them what to do when they feel violent and then help them with their feelings.

EIGHT-YEAR-OLD GIRL:

Why is there violence?

There is violence because people are sometimes jealous of each other.

Why are people violent?

People are violent because they see other people doing it.

What do you think we can do about violence?

Have a secret video camera that sees violence and catches people, and the people get punished.

TEN-YEAR-OLD GIRL:

Why is there violence?

One reason there is war and violence is this: I have a brother. He might say something kind of insulting to me. Then I might shove him. Then he could shove me back. Then maybe I'd punch him. Then he'd punch me. Then I'd trip him and he would fall over and cry. Often, this is basically how war works.

Why are people violent?

There are many reasons that people are violent. One is that people are mad at other people. Another is that people are just out of control. Yet another is that people are unhappy and blame others for their misfortune. One more is that people are obsessed with violence.

What do you think we can do about violence?

We can lessen the amount of violence in the world by learning to control our emotions.

NINE-YEAR-OLD GIRL:

What is violence?

Violence is not treating someone good.

Why are people violent?

People are violent because they feel bad about themselves.

What do you think we can do about violence?

Give them something else to do.

EIGHT-YEAR-OLD BOY:

Why is there violence?

I think there is violence because people get so mad and worked up they get violent.

Why are people violent?

I think there are people who are violent because they may be on drugs.

What do you think we can do about violence?

Try to stop the violence when we see it.

EIGHT-YEAR-OLD BOY:

Why is there violence?

Because some people like to do crazy stuff like bomb threats and fires and lots of stuff.

Why are people violent?

Because of killing.

What do you think we can do about violence?

Not being violent, no killing, no bomb threats, no fires, no pushing or shoving.

EIGHT-YEAR-OLD BOY:

Why is there violence?
   Because there are bomb threats.
Why are people violent?
   Because of killing.

What do you think we can do about violence?
   Just stop it.

EIGHT-YEAR-OLD BOY:

Why is there violence?
   Because people are violent and people see other people. Because someone kills someone's friend and so they kill them.

Why are people violent?
   Because people kill other people.
What do you think we can do about violence?
   Don't do it in the first place, then there will be no violence.

EIGHT-YEAR-OLD BOY:

Why is there violence?
   Because they want to.
Why are people violent?
   I don't know.

What do you think we can do about violence?
   Stop it.

NINE-YEAR-OLD GIRL:

Why is there violence?

There is violence because some people get drunk and fight for no reason.

Why are people violent?

People are violent because if someone got murdered they would want to do that.

What do you think we can do to stop violence?

What I think would stop violence is if we reduce the sale of liquor products.

EIGHT-YEAR-OLD BOY:

Why is there violence?

Because people tease each other.

Why do you think people are violent?

They get violent to win them over.

What do you think we can do about violence?

If the people who were being violent knew it didn't do any good.

NINE-YEAR-OLD GIRL:

Why is there violence?

I think there is violence because so many people argue over such little things and make mole hills into mountains and people fight and sometimes get killed.

Why are people violent?

I think people get violent partly because of drugs and people might get drunk and get violent. Or somebody might think that it would be cool if they hurt someone. *What do you think we can do about violence?*

I think we could help stop violence by not taking so many drugs and stop fighting for the fun of it.

NINE-YEAR-OLD BOY:

Why is there violence?

I think there is violence because people get things and other people want them and they ask. The other people say no and they fight for it.

Why are people violent?

I think people are violent because of drugs and alcohol.

What do you think we can do about violence?

If someone wants something you can give part of it to them and tell them where they can get it, except if it's nuclear.

NINE-YEAR-OLD GIRL:

Why is there violence?

There is violence because some people want something and the way they can get it is to hurt or even kill someone or something. There is also violence because some people are crazy or take drugs.

What do you think we can do about violence?

I think what we can do about it is not take drugs and enjoy what we have and we can together find ways to have what we need so we will be happy and not want what other people have as much. We can use words to solve problems.

TEN-YEAR-OLD GIRL:

Why is there violence?

There is violence because people don't think and they don't use their minds the way they should. They watch violent TV and movies and get addicted to that and start doing violence themselves.

Why are people violent?

People are violent because they can't control themselves.

What do you think we can do about violence?

We can sue all the violent movie makers.

TEN-YEAR-OLD BOY:

Why is there violence?

Because people don't get what they want and hate each other.

Why are people violent?

Because they hate each other and think other colored people are weird.

What do you think we can do about violence?

You should tell your teacher, mother and father how good you feel about that person.

TEN-YEAR-OLD GIRL:

Why is there violence?

Maybe it's because some people are just really hateful and they are really messed up and they blame others for their own faults.

Why are people violent?

Some people enjoy others getting hurt or they are messed up.

What do you think we can do about violence?

Convince violent people that it isn't right to hurt or kill other people and discourage other people from starting to be violent.

TEN-YEAR-OLD GIRL:

Why is there violence?

Because some people think violence is the only way to solve fights.

Why are people violent?

They can't deal with their anger by themselves.

What do you think we can do about violence?

Teach people not to do wrong.

TEN-YEAR-OLD GIRL:

Why is there violence?

I think there is violence because ever since the war (the world war) started they thought they should start fighting.

Why are people violent?

Because they see other people fighting so they think they should start.

What do you think we can do about violence?

If you are fighting with someone, you should stop fighting because there is no point in fighting because it's stupid, you don't need to fight. You can get what you want without fighting. If there is something that you want, you should check with the other person to see if it is okay with them. If they don't agree then you should find something you both agree on.

TEN-YEAR-OLD GIRL:

Why is there violence?
Because people do not understand each other.
Why are people violent?
Because they want to understand.

What do you think we can do about violence?
Try to make people understand.

TEN-YEAR-OLD GIRL:

Why is there violence?
Some people get upset at something or someone and like to let their feeling out in a bad way. Some people think it's a joke.

Why are people violent?
There is violence because people are violent.
What do you think we can do about violence?
We can not be violent and people will copy us.

TEN-YEAR-OLD BOY:

Why is there violence?
I think there is violence because people are sad or mad and they want to take it out on someone else or they think they are powerful enough to take over other countries.

What do you think we can do about violence?
We can write a letter but it wouldn't do any good.

TEN-YEAR-OLD GIRL:

Why is there violence?

Sometimes somebody tells somebody to kill someone and they tell them that they'll give you money or something.

What do you think we can do about violence?

I think if there wasn't violence people wouldn't have to go to jail. So if people stop being violent then the world would.

Achieving Emotional Balance, Healthy Values and Strong Communities

"Interdependence is a fundamental law of nature. Many of the smallest insects are social beings who, without any religion, law, or education, survive by mutual cooperation based on an innate recognition of their inter-connectedness."

—THE DALAI LAMA

I vividly recall the day that I began to experience concern regarding the future of community life. It was March 13, 1964, and I was barely seventeen. Some of my friends and I were eating lunches out of paper bags in my prized fifty-dollar 1950 blue Studebaker. We were listening to a new Elvis song. A news report interrupted the music: *"Shortly after 3:00 A.M., Kitty Genovese, a twenty-eight-year-old bar manager, was walking toward her home from work and was attacked. For almost an hour, thirty-eight respectable, law-abiding citizens in Queens, New York, watched a killer stalk and stab Miss Genovese in three separate attacks. . . ."*

I can remember feeling shock, immediate denial and rationalization: "That could only happen in New York City. It could never happen here." During the next several months, I became obsessed with the Kitty Genovese murder. I read everything I could find. It became the focus of written assignments. A woman had been raped and then killed in full view of members of her own community. People watched the attack for almost an hour and didn't help her. It's interesting to me now that the news report had such an impact on my young life. I experienced trauma daily in my home. My parents were alcoholic and abusive. My mother made repeated threats of suicide during my years growing up. My father, a survivor of World War II and the Korean War, suffered what I now know as post-traumatic stress disorder, reliving the war in graphic detail when he was drunk.

By the time I was seventeen, I had fully experienced the trauma of growing up in a painful family and painful world. I understood the terror of war and was horrified that a Hitler could exist and that people would view such a man as a leader. I was aware of the Cold War with Russia and the impending threat of full-scale war.

Like so many of the youth in the sixties, I prayed for peace. I watched the brutal race riots in Mississippi in 1962 on the six o'clock news and prayed for lasting human rights. I had experienced the tragic deaths of two junior high school friends and learned too early that young life was tenuous. I had been the one to announce the assassination of President John F. Kennedy to my high school classmates, and we mourned with a nation. I witnessed the killing of Lee Harvey Oswald on national television as I questioned my belief about justice. By the time I was seventeen, I had become fully acquainted with grief and trauma. That day in March of my junior year in high school, I experienced an almost greater fear: the unsettling isolation and sense of disconnection that comes with the first full awareness of community apathy.

Although all of my grandparents had died before I was born and I had little contact with extended family, I experienced the support and love of a second cousin, and countless adopted aunts, uncles, adoptive grandparents, elders and teachers. Like most children of military parents, I moved several times early in life, but there were always individuals in every small town in which I lived that gave warmth and kindness to a hurting little girl. I remember them all well.

As is typical with so many children in pain-filled families, I was protective of my parents and I feared being taken away. I told only one person about the abuses in my family, a Native American elder who reached out to me and who I credit with emotionally and spiritually saving my life. He offered guidance and protection. He offered me an honest mirror through which I was able to see the strength of my spirit. He helped me to understand the pain in my family and the strength and values that can come from extended family and community. I have tried to pass these values on to my children.

There were countless other community members along the way who offered warmth and attention and gave me a sense of importance and value in the world: Those who allowed me to recognize my self-worth, mentored me in life skills, listened to my ideas and taught me about healthy emotion. An older man and his wife invited me to work with them on their ranch and taught me about the importance of interdependency and hard work. Even the ranch dog was a respected worker and was considered an important part of the whole. Another neighbor owned horses, taught me to ride and gave me my own horse. He became a loving elder. Five teachers along the way showed me how to value my creativity. They gave merit to the sensitivity I showed concerning the effects of war and racial discrimination. These people shared more than skills; they shared themselves.

Even though I experienced a world of trauma throughout my childhood, I also experienced the love and compassion of emotionally healthy community members who took the time for a child and became an extended family. They were positive models from whom I learned values and with whom I could gaze into clear mirrors. I experienced connection and hope, as well as a glimpse of my role and responsibility as an adult and elder. My awareness of the communal response to the brutal rape and murder of Kitty Genovese threatened my solid beliefs about the enduring foundations of the community life that I valued and depended on for my future children.

Rights Without Responsibilities

The civil rights movement of the sixties paved the way to a new sense of freedom for the oppressed people throughout the nation. The nation finally began honoring the equality of African Americans and women. We also witnessed essential changes in children's rights and the rights of employees. An oppressive society began to be challenged and altered.

As we move toward 2000, however, our fixation on individual rights has begun to damage the fabric of community. We have moved from "we" to "me." John Leo, an associate professor of English at the University of Rhode Island, wrote, "American politics is awash in rights . . . the right to own an AK-47 for hunting purposes, the right not to be tested for AIDS and the right not to inform anyone we may be infecting. According to the ACLU, airline pilots have a right not to be randomly tested for alcohol, leaving passengers with an implied right to crash every now and then. . . . Defining and protecting rights is important in any political culture, but this culture has reached the point where the obsession with individual rights is making it hard for us to think socially." (1993, pp. 29-30)

Perhaps our increasing focus on individual rights is only clouding the real issue. Have we substituted increased individual rights for the development of healthy values regarding others, and thereby sacrificed responsibility and accountability in the process?

BIGGER AND MORE, BUT IS IT BETTER?

If we question what was going on in the minds and hearts of Kitty Genovese's neighbors on March 13, 1964, we may begin to at least partially understand the learned helplessness that has become epidemic in many communities since that time.

The lack of response was far more complex than people merely not wanting to get involved. Many said they thought "someone else would help." Some thought it was a matter for the police that didn't concern them. Some felt helpless.

Individuals have become increasingly dependent on social services and other government agencies to take control of the problems that exist within their neighborhoods and communities. When we become dependent on government intervention, we frequently become disempowered. We begin to give up and become apathetic in determining our own destiny. When we are dependent and disempowered, we often turn to blaming and become angry as well: "Let them handle it." "They always mess up, it's not my fault." "They're in charge. It wasn't any of my business."

In a more recent example of the apathy that characterized the response to the Kitty Genovese assault, people were disgusted and shocked by the behavior of a young man who recently stood idly outside the door of a casino restroom while his friend was sexually assaulting and killing a seven-year-old child. Reportedly, when he was asked how he felt regarding the public's outrage, he replied, "I'm not losing any sleep over it. The notoriety is getting me more dates."

The lack of concern and subsequent arrogance in this young man about the death of a seven-year-old child seems astounding. Yet thousands of adults witness violence every day and do nothing. Their responses when asked why they didn't try to offer assistance or call for help is generally, "It wasn't any of my business. I didn't want to get involved."

The young man's outlook, although terrifying, isn't terribly uncommon. The outrage experienced by so many regarding this incident might not only reflect the attitude toward his uncaring and apathetic lack of response, but also at the mirror he so blatantly holds up for all of us. His lack of community values are the product of our apathetic society.

Since World War II, state and federal agencies have largely taken the place of people helping people. Many individuals and smaller private institutions no longer believe that they have anything to offer. People have told me they didn't take action when they heard the screams of a woman or a child because to do so might "cause them trouble," or they "might do something wrong." I have heard countless times that people didn't help because they weren't "qualified" to offer assistance.

One woman at a conference spoke to me about a neighbor who was being physically abused nearly every week by an adult son. The neighbor in question was seventy years old. The woman said, "Well, yes, I know her, but what could I say? I'm not a professional. I would probably say the wrong thing. Maybe she would think that what's going on in her house is none of my business."

With the increase in federal and state agencies has come mountains of paper work, forms, catchment areas, departments, codes, classifications and restrictions, laws, rights, violations, suits, lawyers, and, of course, technicalities.

Very early in my career, a pregnant woman with a one-year-old child came to see me for support and counseling. Her husband had been abusing her, and she had courageously taken her son and left with little more than the clothes on their backs. She had found an inexpensive apartment for her and her son and had been promised a job. That job had fallen through. She had been promised another job but it wasn't due to start for a week.

She had gone to several public agencies seeking financial assistance. She did not want welfare, just food for a couple of weeks. She had been told by each agency that she didn't quite meet their qualifications for short-term assistance: she hadn't been out of work long enough or hadn't been in the state long enough. Another told her she'd have to wait fourteen days, to which she replied, "I won't need it then."

She saw me for the first time after waiting all day at one agency. I suggested that she talk to the small grocer a short ways from her apartment. This family store had been in the community forever. When I was pregnant with my first son and my car was broken down, they had insisted on carrying groceries two blocks to my house. When the store owners heard the young woman's story, they immediately offered to help: "Of course we will help. Would you like to just run a tab until you start working? Many people need to on occasion. We also have some things we might just be able to let you have. Welcome to the community. Those people you're going to start working for are good people. They'll treat you right."

Neighborhood grocers, like the one that came to this woman's assistance, are a relic in many communities. They are being run out of business by corporate chains that can buy in bulk and charge less for their products. Neighborhood businesses need the support of their communities to stay in business. The value of small businesses frequently extends much farther than the products they sell. Supporting small business by paying a few cents extra is usually worth the investment.

AWAY FROM THE FRONT STOOP

One afternoon I was having a discussion with my husband, who had grown up in a major metropolitan area and had worked early in his career as a counselor with violent gangs in New York City. I had grown up in the country and was interested in his thoughts about the changing sense of community in large urban areas. He said, "Things changed a lot when huge housing projects were built and people left their front stoops. Among other things, crime began to steadily increase."

I learned that sociologists actually had a name for this aspect of life in large cities: "Front Stoop Neighborhood Control." In the fifties and earlier, family life in cities used to encompass sitting out on the front stoops of apartment buildings and small houses during all hours of the day and evening. Families socialized and swapped stories about the old country, earlier days, and the difficulties of city life, or shared the most current information about children or families. They also kept an eye on neighborhood children and were acutely aware of the comings and goings of people on their block. When the huge new building projects were constructed after World War II, front stoops became less common, and a very important and necessary aspect of community life in the cities disappeared.

Suburban homeowners built fences both literally and

figuratively. Neighbors began fencing themselves in and adjoining families out. Fences and other obstructions to communication became more imposing over the years as fear in communities increased. People began demanding more privacy. Isolation increased and conversations decreased. Arguments between neighbors began to flourish over whose dog was on whose lawn, who paints and repairs the fence, whose children were running through the yards, who was acceptable in the neighborhood, or who was going to sue whom over what.

Interestingly enough, police, crime prevention specialists and concerned citizens throughout the country are trying to encourage neighbors to recreate Front Stoop Neighborhood Control in the form of Neighborhood Watches or Block Watches. Police officers are encouraging people to lower their fences, cut shrubs and trees in front of windows, and begin to watch out for one another. Block watches have proven successful in moving crime out of neighborhoods. The success of a block watch rests in the fact that as communication between neighbors increase, people become more aware of each other. People get to know each other and, in that knowing, begin to feel a new sense of responsibility for each other. It's interesting to note that the once so natural values of connection that have been mentioned so many times in this book today have to be legislated.

LEARNING TO SPEAK THE TRUTH

Coal miners a long time ago practiced a certain survival custom. They would always take a canary with them into the mines.

If the canary became ill and began to die, the miners would know that a toxic odorless gas had seeped into the mine that would eventually cause a decrease in the oxygen supply. If we take the time to listen to children and youth, and really see what is happening today, we will become immediately aware that our children are the canaries in our communities.

In the past several years, I have worked with a large number of communities all over the world. Most of the time, requests for my assistance result directly from messages sent by children and youth—delivered either through their deaths or the painful quality of their lives. The powerful truth of their message usually begins to wake people up.

Dr. Angeles Arrien, in her book *The Four-Fold Way: Walking the Paths of the Warrior, Teacher, Healer & Visionary*, speaks to the need for individuals to begin to "speak the truth without blame or judgment." Learning to speak the truth responsibly, without blame, is essential for communities to start the restoration process.

I recently was asked to intervene in a community that had experienced a dramatic increase in adult violence as well as developing gang activity and suicides among the youth. I often arrive in an area the day before my community workshop is to begin. While wandering through this particular town, I was impressed by the number and variety of beautiful posters hanging in stores, schools, and the post office, on utility poles and in other public locations. They spoke to many themes, "Take the Time to Help a Child," "There Is No Excuse for Domestic Violence," "Help Us All Prevent Abuse to Our Children," "A Friend Doesn't Let a Friend Drive Drunk," etc.

During the workshop the next day I mentioned the pretty posters and asked if their themes were the real norms of the community. I explained that norms were the unspoken rules that people in groups follow. They all laughed and said an emphatic "No!" I asked the group to help me list the real rules of their community on large pieces of newsprint throughout the room.

The youth were the first to respond. They all agreed that the pretty posters had nothing to do with the way people functioned. Some of the community norms they listed were: "Do as I Say, Not as I Do!"; "Go with the Power, Right or Wrong"; "Please Those in Power"; "Don't Talk to Anyone About Anything Important"; "Mind Your Own Business"; "Gossip Is the Common Truth"; "That Doesn't Happen in My Community"; "Don't Feel, Use Alcohol and Drugs"; "It's My Way or the Highway"; "It's O.K. to Hit as Long as You're Bigger"; "Entertain Yourself, We're Busy," etc.

Before the end of the week, the youth decided to replace the pretty posters with the real ones. On the top of each they wrote, "It's Time to Speak the Truth." Some people were upset by the posters, but it did wake them up. One woman said, "It's about time we woke up. We've been asleep too long. Sometimes it takes the young ones to tell the truth. I don't know about anyone else, but I'd much rather them tell us while they're alive than tell us through their dying." Frequently when working with communities, I divide the large group into smaller groups, asking each to build their community as they see it. I provide the materials to complete the task. Each group is to show how they perceive people working or not working together, barriers to communication in the community, and the power structures that exist.

After the small groups have completed the task, they share with the larger group their perceptions of the community by sharing the structures they have built. We fully examine blocks in communication and misuses of power. Community members offer creative approaches that can be instrumental in rebuilding a community that supports the health of its members.

Usually the walls between one another have been built from unresolved conflicts, family feuds, secrets, mistakes in perception, lack of real knowledge, racism, sexism, past violence or gossip. Even though a circle is far stronger than a pyramid, the structures presented almost always indicate top-down misuses of power, rather than empowerment.

Many youth of the community are again the first to speak the truth; they often show, in the sculptures they build, the locations of every drug pusher or crack house, safe and unsafe houses, perpetrators of all types of abuse, as well as individuals who have served as the "natural helpers" of the community. In many years of doing this work, I've found youth are typically the only ones to point out the cemetery and the people they have lost through addictions, suicide, senseless violence, abuses of power, power struggles and community apathy.

Before I leave each community, I often ask the youth to elect four adult community models that they are willing to follow. Young people always choose people that walk their talk. I am continually impressed by the honesty of the youth and their commitment to making responsible and informed decisions. As one young man told me, "We have the most to lose by things staying the way they have been."

The youth in the community escort their four selected models to the center of the circle and, one by one, community members honor the rarely recognized individuals for the gifts that they have given. There are no grand prizes, no money awards. The tears of pride in the eyes of these adults and their expressions of joy come from the validation and respect given to them by their community. The respect shown by the youth for their values and commitment is worth far more to them than money, status or power.

STANDING UP OUR RELATIVES

Many Native American and First Nations elders refer to a time when people knew the importance of "standing each other up," or "staking each other down," which simply means standing together, never letting anyone stand alone. In the circle of community we are all relatives, members of the human race, working side by side and needing support for one another. Yet, over the decades, the circle has slowly broken down and reformed into a pyramid, disconnecting and disempowering us. A child being abused in public is often ignored and the screams of many elderly go unheard.

In one community, a sixteen-year-old girl stood with an older woman on each side, appearing to hold her up. Tears streaming down her face, she told members of her community, for the first time, about the sexual abuse she had suffered from a teacher in the elementary school. As she talked, more and more youth, women and men from the community came to stand with her, lending her their support. Other young people began to speak, also acknowledging for the first time that they were victims of this teacher. It was the first time this community, which had recently endured the pain of many adolescent suicides, faced together the knowledge of a secret that had kept them separated for so long. It was also the first time many were able to grieve the loss of the many young people that had committed suicide. The young woman also was able to share the grief about her best friend, who had recently died in a single-car crash under the influence of drugs and alcohol. She said that her friend had also been a victim of the same teacher.

One man asked, "Why did it take so long for us to stand to-gether? How has this 'secret' been kept so long?" When communities' members disconnect from one another, they often empower hate groups and perpetrators of abuse, who depend on the disconnection between people to continue their activities.

In a peaceful community in Washington state, a hate group attempted to drive out and intimidate people of color. However, people stood together and made it clear that there was no room in their community for hate. The hate group didn't disband; they just moved to another community where the citizens were disconnected enough that the group could gain a foothold and power.

In another community, a veteran of the Vietnam War was invited to guide the community through an ancient ceremony from his culture that welcomed home those who had been to war. The men and women stood together, veterans of World War II, Korea, Vietnam and the Gulf War. Tears that had never been cried streamed down the faces as the veterans held each other up, as one community member after another came up to welcome them home. It seemed that the grief was endless, and—at the end, without a word being spoken—many things became crystal clear. One woman with tears running down her face, having just welcomed her grieving father home, said, "Why couldn't this have happened when he first came back from Korea? Where was the community then? Now I can feel why I grew up in a war zone." Another young man said, "I never realized how much we needed each other. She has lived right next door for years and years and I had no idea how much pain she still carried from Korea. We could have supported one another. Why wasn't this very simple 'Welcome Home' done earlier? Not some ticker-tape parade in New York or Washington, D.C., but with our own community. How have we become so isolated from one another?"

Television shows like *Picket Fences* and *Northern Exposure* soared to the top of the ratings because most of us are drawn to the idea of community: The local judge modeling values and wisdom, the general practice doctor who knows the family, the local grocer who is willing to run a tab and community members of all professions and backgrounds struggling together on behalf of children, against the tides of change and the values in the fast lane . . . these are the images we cherish. One woman sadly told me, "Do you remember when we used to get caught up in movies about science fiction? I think we did because the life that was portrayed was so unreal. Now I think we get caught up in shows like *Picket Fences* because the community values it portrayed are now like a fantasy, a lost world far away that many of us want back but don't know how to find."

We see interdependence immediately coming into place again during times of crisis. How many volunteered to help after the Oklahoma City bombing or in times of natural disaster? People have a life-preserving instinct to connect. They feel good about having something to offer and coming to the aid of others in need. Individuals again feel connected, empowered, accountable to one another, a part of the whole again. Is it that simple? We rush to the support of one another when we again know that we have something valuable to offer. The response to community crisis shows our desire to stand by our neighbors.

ACHIEVING BALANCE

One powerful indicator of a desire to connect is the incredible response to Internet chat rooms and forums. Yet despite many opinions to the contrary, I don't believe sitting at a computer terminal and typing words in cyberspace is going to help us stand by one another and rebuild communities. It wouldn't have helped the girl who died keeping the secret of sexual abuse in the community and wouldn't have provided those veterans a welcoming. The Internet offers a feeble attempt to relate when we have otherwise suffered the loss of the natural laws of interconnectedness; you can still turn the computer on and shut it off again like a light switch whenever you want, without ever facing another human being. Chat rooms speak to the need people have to connect, yet the imposing technology still highlights lives out of balance.

The technology itself is not the problem. The Internet, for instance, allows a tremendous amount of knowledge to be collected from experts all over the world in a very short period of time. Video games like the Mario Brothers or Tetris can teach problem-solving skills and spatial relations. If you spend all your spare time on a computer, however, and neglect needs for physical exercise and connection to others, your life is out of balance. In a similar way, if you spend most of your free time compulsively exercising, or even spend the majority of time attending self-help meetings, your life is out of balance.

Many years ago, Harold Belmont—a Native American elder, spiritual leader, trainer and consultant—taught a useful tool that helps individuals regularly evaluate the degree of balance in their lives. The tool is based on the centuries-old Native American medicine wheel.

There are four quadrants on the wheel: mental, emotional, spiritual and physical. For the purposes of self-evaluation, Harold instructed that each of the four lines that separate the quadrants be broken into ten segments. The idea is to evaluate oneself in each area, starting at the center and moving out. For instance, if you spend a great deal of time in mental activity, reading, school work, working on a computer or intellectualizing, you might rate yourself high mentally, perhaps an eight. You would therefore put a dot on the eighth space on the quadrant line relating to mental.

Before undertaking the task of evaluating yourself, further definition in each area might be useful:

Mental
The time you spend in mental activity. Mental focus globally has resulted in a great deal of technological advancement.

Emotional
Achieving emotional balance means the ability to experience an entire range of emotional expression. Individuals that have emotional competency can allow themselves to be dependent sometimes as well as being independent. They experience their emotions in the present. They cry when they are sad and laugh

when they are happy. They have a sense of humor. Emotionally competent individuals express anger productively rather than the expression being destructive to self or others.

When evaluating yourself, you might ask yourself: "Do I smile when I am angry or sad? Do I become rageful or hostile when I feel vulnerable? Do I cry when I'm really angry? Am I always gloomy or do I have equal periods of joy? Do I blame others when things go wrong? Do I allow myself to make mistakes? Are there long periods of time when I feel numb?"

In evaluating yourself in this area, you might consider whether you are in a period of growth or if you've been at a standstill for a while. For instance, a person might spend a great deal of time going to support groups or going to counseling, yet may be stuck in anger after years of focus on emotional health. That same individual may have said that they've "forgiven" their abuser early in their personal work, yet may still feel pain in their stomach every time they encounter the individual.

Spiritual

Spiritual competency means connection. Do you feel connection with others or do you feel isolated? Are you active in your community? Do you feel a connection to your cultural heritage? Do you feel comfortable giving and being given to? Do you spend time alone as well as with others? Do you feel comfortable asking for what you need as well as responding to the needs of others?

Physical

Living in physical balance means paying attention to your body. For example: Are you sick more than you're healthy? Do you drink alcohol to excess? Do you smoke? Do you use drugs? Do you exercise? Do you eat foods that help or foods that harm? Is your diet balanced? Do you maintain a weight that is healthy for you? Do you sleep well or do you awaken tired? Do you practice preventive health?

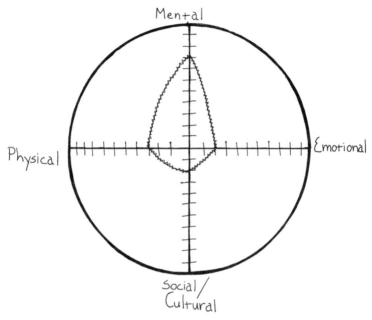

Belmont suggests that it is useful to evaluate yourself and also have a friend evaluate you on a separate piece of paper. The individual you choose might also perform a self-evaluation and have you evaluate her or him. The person you select should be someone who knows you well and will not have difficulty giving you honest feedback. After you and your chosen partner in this exercise have evaluated yourselves and each other, share your perceptions. After you have marked each area, connect the markings. Does it make a circle? Are you in balance or is your life out of balance? Does your perception of yourself agree with your partner's? What have you learned?

After the exercise, the key is to put time and energy into areas that are rated low. Many who have difficulty living in balance might find this exercise a useful daily tool. Awareness in the four areas becomes automatic after a while and can aid a person in staying focused on balance. While initially learning about life balance, it would be important to do this exercise weekly in a journal so that you can see the progress you are making. Sharing evaluations with another could take place every other week.

Try evaluating our world and our society in these areas. When we are able to see things from this perspective, understanding why individual lives are out of balance becomes easier. When individuals are out of balance, it affects the broader society, and imbalance in society in turn influences the lives of individuals.

CHANGE

The tide is slowly shifting toward the rebuilding of communities. As people truly see what is happening in their communities, they have become more ready to accept discomfort and work toward change. An excellent example of a changing trend was the Million Man March on Washington, D.C., on October 16, 1996. Although many still focus on the pros and cons of the organizers—Rev. Louis Farrakhan and the Rev. Benjamin Chavis—or the idea that the march was exclusively for black men, the importance of the experience for thousands of African-American families and communities cannot be minimized. Many still talk about the tears in men's eyes as they proudly marched on our nation's capital and pledged to change themselves for future generations. The march was not Farrakhan's, it was theirs.

Far too many times, significant changes in communities become politicized to the extent we lose the impact on people. In a 1997 article on America Online, Melinda Beck reported, "Former 'Crip' Charles Rachal and former 'Blood' Leon Gulette took a commercial flight home together, sharing ideas for getting other young hoods away from gang life. . . ." Beck also wrote that, "Detroit Mayor Dennis Archer came home from the march ready to take on the Devil. By long-standing tradition, the night before Halloween brings out mayhem in Motown. Last year's vandals celebrated 'Devil's Night' by setting more than one hundred fires throughout the city. This year Archer appealed for calm in the spirit of the Million Man March. By midweek, 15,000 people had called into the city's help line, volunteering to prevent fires and to combat violence and enforce a municipal curfew."

These are only two changes that were influenced by men standing together. By overcoming our communal sense of learned helplessness, we can begin to "stand each other up."

Many politicians have felt the gradual shift that is taking place in the hearts of people who are recognizing the importance of making the shift from "me" to "we." Campaign speeches promise renewed family values and the creation of safe communities. But politicians can't legislate changes in values, and the rebuilding of communities can't come from campaign promises. These changes will come from people in communities who recognize that we needn't wait for a crisis to come together. Besides, in many ways the crisis is already here. Children that are the canaries in society's mines are reminding us that we have a lot of work to do. They are our messengers. Children are warning us by their actions and, far too often, by their deaths.

CREATING A VISION

Many of us learned throughout the 1950s and 1960s that a movement must have a vision. In order to move the present toward a healthy future, we must not only know what we are against, but also what we support. Too often people expend a great deal of energy complaining about relationships, the way others treat them, politics, the state of health care.... I usually ask, "What ideas do you have that you believe will make a difference? How much time and energy are you willing to commit to actualize your vision? How can I help?" Most of the time my questions are answered with uncomfortable silence.

If our imaginations are limited to continued illness, unhappy relationships, depression, isolation and degradation, we shouldn't be surprised when we live what we imagine. All of us at times have been guilty of complaining about a relationship, our health, lack of values in our youth, or the government. Too often, we blame others, expecting them to change things for us, then we complain about the actions that were taken and feel angry when things stay the same.

By creating visions of how we want our personal lives to be and then branching out to how we want our communities and society to act, we begin to move toward the positive goals of emotional health in all areas of our lives. When we achieve that health, we'll find ourselves in balance.

APPENDIX: MEDICATIONS FOR EFFECTIVE TREATMENT OF DEPRESSION

I have many reasons for objecting to the treatment of depression with medications only. One is that in our "better-world-through-chemistry" society, we begin to believe that we are personally far removed from the changes that are occurring in our psychological, emotional and physical beings. "Change just happened. I had no control over it. I certainly didn't make it happen."

Frequently I ask people to make lists of the areas in their lives where they believe they influence their own destiny. I also ask them to make a list of areas in their lives where they believe they have no control. We then go over the lists together and begin to work on ways the individual can feel more influence over parts of their lives as well as feel a sense of competency in areas where they do feel influence. "I can't" becomes a phrase used less frequently as time goes on. After I spoke with my newly found friend at the bank machine, he decided to get his cash during the week when he could talk with a "real person." He also decided to insist upon being connected with a real person at another company where he was feeling frustration. Just because technology has made the machines available doesn't mean we have to use them. We have choice. We don't have to be prisoners to technology. The same holds true for a purely medicinal approach to depression.

In many cases, the temporary use of medication is a necessary part of effective treatment for depression. Medication changes your biochemistry but does not solve your problems. Nonetheless, several categories of medications are effective in the treatment of depression. Sometimes one medication is not effective, but another might be more useful in your particular case.

Tricyclic Medications

Some of the tricyclic medications are Tofranil (imipramine), Norpramin (desipramine), Elavil (amitriptyline), Anafranil (clomipramine) and Pamelor (nortriptyline). It is wise to understand that medications change often, and that it is impossible to list all of them.

One of the common biochemical reasons for depression is that reuptake becomes too eager, depleting the amount of neurotransmitters available for use. Tricyclic medications interfere with enthusiastic reuptake. They block the ability of the nerve cells to recycle the neurotransmitters, thereby inhibiting reuptake.

Second-Generation Antidepressants

Many of you are familiar with the names of the second generation of antidepressant medications: Prozac (fluoxetine), Zoloft (sertraline), Paxil (paroxetine), Desyrel (trazodone), Serzone (nefazodone), Effexor (venlafaxine), Luvox (fluvoxamine) and Wellbutrin (bupropion).

Like tricyclics, the second-generation antidepressants change the amount of neurotransmitters between nerve cells. Serotonergic agents block recycling of serotonin just like most tricyclics block the reuptake of norepinephrine (although some block the uptake of serotonin as well).

Generally, second-generation antidepressants have fewer side effects than tricyclics, but that isn't necessarily the case for some people. It is vitally important that you go over all medications with your physician.

MAO Inhibitors (Monoamine Oxidase Inhibitors)

Nerve cells both make and destroy neurotransmitters internally. Enzymes called monoamine oxidates destroy neurotransmitters. MAO inhibitors basically stop the cells from producing the neurotransmitter-destroying enzymes, thus making more neurotransmitters available. Some commonly prescribed MAO inhibitors are Nardil (phenelzine), Parnate (tranylcypromine) and Marplan (isocarboxazid).

MAO inhibitors are among the earliest medications for depression. They are also probably the most controversial medications prescribed because of their serious side effects when taken in combination with some foods such as cheese, wine, beer, beans, fermented foods, as well as some over-the-counter medications. But taken properly, MAO inhibitors can be as safe as tricyclics.

Alternatives to Prescribed Medication

As mentioned earlier, aerobic exercise changes the body chemistry of depression and can work as a natural antidepressant for some individuals.

Studies have also indicated that changing self-defeating thought processes (negative self-talk) can be instrumental in biochemical changes.

An over-the-counter medication that has become enormously popular over the last few years is St. John's wort. It was originally thought that this herbal extract worked in much the same way as MAO inhibitors. St. John's wort is now thought to work on at least two other mechanisms: inhibition of the reuptake of serotonin and modulation of interleukin-6. Interleukin-6 is heavily involved in the communication between cells.

A Word of Caution

As mentioned earlier, it is vitally important that individuals being treated for depression feel a sense of control over their own destiny. Physicians and counselors should be able to explain the options available and make recommendations for what they believe will be effective treatment. Choice belongs to the individual.

After starting a regime of medication, however, it is imperative to work closely with your doctor. Antidepressant medications cannot just be started and randomly stopped. Also, taking an antidepressant medication and then deciding on your own to change to St. John's wort before the other medication can be gradually decreased can produce "serotonin syndrome." This syndrome is characterized by confusion, fever, sweating, shivering, muscle spasms and diarrhea.

It is my belief that depression is caused by delayed grief, cumulative trauma, environmental stress, self-hate messages, learned helplessness or a combination of two or more of these factors. Biochemistry alone will not work on any one of or a combination of these factors. Taking medication only is a bit like using a bucket to bail water out of a boat in order to stop it from sinking when no one has paid attention to the hole in the side of the boat. Fixing the boat seems too complicated or exhausting. Maybe some tried to fix their boats and the tools they used didn't work. So we just keep bailing out the water. The boat never sinks, but it never stops filling with water either.

WORKS CITED

BOOKS

Abdullah, Sharif M. *The Power of One: Authentic Leadership in Turbulent Times.* Philadelphia: New Society Publishers, 1995.

Akbar, Na'im. *Chains and Images of Psychological Slavery.* Jersey City, New Jersey: New Mind Productions, 1984.

Allcorn, Seth. *Anger in the Workplace: Understanding Aggression and Violence.* Wesport, Ct.: Quorum Books, 1994.

Anonymous. "The Companions of Duty." In *Changing Community (The Graywolf Annual 10).* Scott Walker (Ed.). St. Paul, Minn.: Grey Wolf Press, 1993: 135.

Arrien, Angeles. *The Four-Fold Way: Walking the Paths of the Warrior, Teacher, Healer & Visionary.* San Francisco: HarperCollins, 1993.

Bettelheim, Bruno. *Surviving and Other Essays.* New York: Vintage Books, 1980.

Bowlby, John. *Attachment and Loss: Volume III, Loss, Sadness and Depression.* New York: Basic Books, Inc., 1980.

Bramson, Robert M. *Coping with Difficult People.* New York: Doubleday, Anchor Books, 1981.

Cannon, Walter. *Bodily Changes in Pain: Hunger, Fear and Rage.* New York: Appleton, 1929.

Cousins, Norman. *Anatomy of an Illness.* New York: W. W. Norton and Company, 1979.

Cox, T. "Stress: A Psychophysiological Approach to Cancer." In *Psychosocial Stress and Cancer.* C. L. Cooper (Ed.). New York: John Wiley, 1984: 149-169.

Davis, Angela Yvonne. *Angela Davis: An Autobiography.* New York: International Publishing, 1989.

Derber, Charles. *The Wilding of America: How Greed and Violence are Eroding Our Nation's Character.* New York: St. Martin's Press, 1996.

Dershowitz, Alan M. *The Abuse Excuse: And Other Cop-Outs, Sob Stories, Evasions of Responsibility.* New York: Little, Brown and Company, Backbay Books, 1994.

Dyer, G. *War.* London, England: Guild Publishing, 1985.

Esler, Gavin. *United States of Anger: The People and the American Dream.* New York: Michael Joseph Limited, Penguin Books USA, Inc., 1997.

Ewing, Charles Patrick. *Kids Who Kill.* Lexington, Ky.: Lexington Books, 1990.

Eyre, Linda, and Richard Eyre. *Life Balance: How to Simplify and Bring Harmony to Your Everyday Life.* New York: Simon & Schuster, Fireside, 1997.

Freire, Paulo. *Pedagogy of the Oppressed.* New Revised 20th Anniversary Edition, Translated by Myra Bergman Ramos. New York: Continuum, 1993.

Friedman, Meyer, and Ray Rosenman. *Type A Behavior and Your Heart.* New York: Knopf, 1974.

Gabriel, R. A. *Military Psychiatry: A Comparative Perspective.* New York: Greenport Press, 1986.

Gilligan, James. *Violence: Reflections on a National Epidemic.* New York: Random House, Vintage Books, 1997.

Glasser, William. *Choice Theory: A New Psychology of Personal Freedom.* New York: HarperCollins, 1998.

Grossman, David. *On Killing, The Psychological Cost of Learning to Kill in War and Society.* Boston: Little, Brown, and Company, 1995.

Groth, A. Nicholas, with H. Jean Birnbaum. *Men Who Rape: The Psychology of the Offender.* New York: Plenum Press, 1979.

Haynal, Andre, Miklos Molnar, and Gerard De Puymege. *Fanaticism: A Historical and Psychoanalytical Study.* New York: Schocken Books, 1983.

Huxley, Aldous. *Brave New World.* New York: Bantam, Harper and Brothers, 1939.

Irwin, J., and H. Anisman. "Stress and Pathology: Immunological and Central Nervous System Interactions." In *Psychological Stress and Cancer.* C. L. Cooper (Ed.). New York: John Wiley, 1984.

Jacobson, Neil, and John Gottman. *When Men Batter Women: New Insights into Ending Abusive Relationships.* New York: Simon & Schuster, 1998.

Jamison, Kaleel. *The Nibble Theory and the Kernel of Power. A Book About Leadership, Self-Empowerment, and Personal Growth.* Mahwah, N.J.: Paulist Press, 1984.

Jensen, Jean C. *Reclaiming Your Life: A Step-by-Step Guide to Using Regression Therapy to Overcome the Effects of Childhood Abuse.* Hammondsworth, Middlesex, England: Dutton, 1995.

Kang, H. S. *Dong Yang Euitiak Gaeron (Introduction to East Asian Medicine).* Seoul: Komun-sa, 1981.

Lamb, Sharon. *The Trouble with Blame: Victims, Perpetrators and Responsibility.* Cambridge, Mass.: Harvard University Press, 1996.

Lawrence, Marilyn, ed. *Fed Up and Hungry: Women, Oppression and Food.* New York: Peter Bedrick Books, 1987.

Lee, S. H. *In This Earth and That Wind: This Is Korea.* D. I. Steinberg (Trans.). Seoul: Hollym. Corp., 1967.

Lefkowitz, Bernard. *Our Guys.* New York: Random House, Vintage Books, 1997.

Leo, John. "Community and Personal Duty." In *Changing Community (The Graywolf Annual 10).* Scott Walker (Ed.). St. Paul, Minn. Grey Wolf Press, 1993: 29–32.

Lerner, Harriet Goldhor. *The Dance of Intimacy.* New York: Harper and Row, 1989.

Lerner, Michael. *Surplus Powerlessness.* Oakland, Calif.: The Institute for Labor and Mental Health, 1986.

Lewis, Dorothy Otnow. *Guilty by Reason of Insanity: A Psychiatrist Explores the Minds of Killers.* New York: Random House, Ballantine Books, 1998.

Louv, Richard. *Childhood's Future.* New York: Anchor Books, 1990.

Lorenz, Konrad. *On Aggression.* London, England: Methuen and Company, 1967.

Marshall, S. L. A. *Men Against Fire.* Gloucester, Mass.: Peter Smith, 1978.

McKay, Matthew, Peter Rogers, and Judith McKay. *When Anger Hurts: Quieting the Storm Within.* Oakland, Calif.: New Harbinger Publications, 1989.

McKay, Matthew, Patrick Fanning, Kim Paleg, and Dana Landis. *When Anger Hurts Your Kids: A Parent's Guide.* New York: MJF Books, 1996.

Medina, John. *Depression: How It Happens, How It's Healed.* Oakland, Calif.: CME, Inc., New Harbinger, 1998.

Middelton-Moz, Jane. *Children of Trauma: Rediscovering Your Discarded Self.* Deerfield Beach, Fla.: Health Communications, Inc., 1989.

———. *Shame and Guilt: Master of Disguise.* Deerfield Beach, Fla.: Health Communications, Inc., 1990.

————. *Will to Survive: Affirming the Positive Power of the Human Spirit.* Deerfield Beach, Fla.: Health Communications, Inc., 1992.

Middelton-Moz, Jane, and Lorie Dwinell. *After the Tears: Reclaiming the Personal Losses of Childhood.* Deerfield Beach, Fla.: Health Communications, Inc., 1986.

Miller, Alice. *The Untouched Key, Tracing Childhood Trauma in Creativity and Destructiveness.* New York: Doubleday, 1988.

Mills, Nicholaus. *The Triumph of Meanness: America's War Against Its Better Self.* Reading, Mass.: Houghton-Mifflin Company, 1997.

Nuckols, Cardwell C., and Bill Chickering. *Healing an Angry Heart: Finding Solace in a Hostile World.* Deerfield Beach, Fla.: Health Communications, 1998.

Ochberg, Frank M. *Post-Traumatic Therapy and Victims of Violence.* New York: Brunner/Mazel, 1988.

Papolos, Demitri, and Janice Papolos. *Overcoming Depression. (3rd ed.)* New York: HarperCollins, 1996.

Pipher, Mary. *The Shelter of Each Other: Rebuilding Our Families.* New York: Ballantine Books, 1996.

Potter-Efron, Ronald. *Angry All the Time: An Emergency Guide to Anger Control.* Oakland, Calif.: New Harbinger Publications, 1994.

Potter-Efron, Ronald, and Patricia Potter-Efron. *Anger, Alcoholism, and Addiction: Treating Individuals, Couples, and Families.* New York: W. W. Norton and Company, 1991.

————. *Letting Go of Anger: The Ten Most Common Anger Styles and What To Do About Them.* Oakland, Calif.: New Harbinger Publications, 1995.

Real, Terrence. *I Don't Want To Talk About It: Overcoming the Secret Legacy of Male Depression.* New York: Simon & Schuster, Fireside, 1997.

Robson, Ruthann. "Marbalo Lesbian Separatism and Neutering Male Cats." In Jess Wells, *Lesbians Raising Sons.* Los Angeles, New York: Alyson Books, 1997.

Roy, Maria, ed. *The Abusive Partner.* New York: Von Nostrand Reinhold Company, 1982.

Rubin, Theodore Isaac. *The Angry Book.* Toronto: The Macmillan Company, 1969.

————. *Compassion and Self-Hate: An Alternative to Despair.* New York: Simon & Schuster, Touchstone, 1998.

Schlessinger, Dr. Laura. *How Could You Do That?! The Abdication of Character, Courage, and Conscience.* New York: HarperPerennial, 1996.

Seligman, Martin E. P. *Helplessness: On Depression, Development, and Death.* New York: W. H. Freeman and Company, 1975.

Seltzer, Mark. *Serial Killers: Death and Life in America's Wounded Culture.* New York: Routledge, 1998.

Shulman, Bernard H. *Contributions to Individual Psychology.* Chicago: Alfred Adler Institute of Chicago, 1973.

Tannen, Deborah. *The Argument Culture: Moving from Debate to Dialogue.* New York: Random House, 1998.

Tavris, Carol. *Anger: The Misunderstood Emotion.* New York: Simon & Schuster, Touchstone, 1982, revised 1989.

Thomas, Sandra, and Cheryl Jefferson. *Use Your Anger: A Woman's Guide to Empowerment.* New York: Simon & Schusterr, Pocket Books, 1996.

Wattenberg, Ben J. *Values Matter Most: How Republicans or Democrats or a Third Party Can Win and Renew the American Way of Life.* New York: Simon & Schuster, The Free Press, 1995.

Wells, Jess, ed. *Lesbians Raising Sons.* Los Angeles: Alyson Publications, 1997.

Williams, Redford, and Virginia Williams. *Anger Kills: Seventeen Strategies for Controlling the Hostility That Can Harm Your Health.* New York: HarperCollins, 1993.

PERIODICALS

Baer, P. E., F. H. Collins, G.C. Bouriano, and M. F. Ketchel. "*Assessing Personality Factors in Essential Hypertension with a Brief Self-Report Instrument.*" Psychosomatic Medicine 7 (1969): pp. 653-659.

Baker, Donald P. "As Kentucky Town Mourns, Movie Suggested as Basis for Boy's Attack." *Washington Post.* December 6, 1997: page A3.

Barefoot, J. C., W. G. Dahlstrom, and R. D. Williams Jr. "Hostility, CHD Incidence, and Total Mortality: A 25-Year Follow-up Study of 255 Physicians." *Psychosomatic Medicine* 45 (1983): pp. 59-63.

Beck, Melinda. "Voices: Food Banks and Marriage Counseling; Marchers Home with Plans to Make a Difference. On America Online, February 4, 1997.

Connell, Dominic, Matthew Joint, and Louis Mizell. "Aggressive Driving: Three Studies," AAA Foundation for Traffic Safety, March 1997.

Cowley, Geoffrey. "Why Children Turn Violent." *Newsweek.* April 6, 1998: pp. 23-26.

Fox, B. H. "The Role of Psychological Factors in Cancer Incidence and Prognosis." *Oncology* 9/3 (1995): pp. 245-253.

Gegax, Trent, Jerry Adler, and Daniel Pedersen. "The Schoolyard Killers: Behind the Ambush." *Newsweek,* April 6, 1998: pp. 19-24.

Grosch, William N. "Shame, Rage and Addiction." *Psychiatric Quarterly* 65/1 (1994): pp. 49-63.

Harburg, E., E. H. Blakelock, and P. J. Roper. "Resentful and Reflective Coping with Arbitrary Authority and Blood Pressure: Detroit." *Psychosomatic Medicine* 41 (1979): pp. 189-202.

Hunt, Steven, and Gina Delmastro. "The Body Cries." *Focus on Family* July/August 1985.

Jensen, R., and J. Shaw "Children as Victims of War: Current Knowledge and Futher Research Needs." *Journal of the American Academy Child Adolescent Psychiatry* 4 (1993): pp. 697-708.

Kaplan, S., L. A. Go, H. S. Chalk, E. Magliocco, D. Rohouit, and W. Ross. "Hostility in Verbal Productions and Hypnotic Dreams in Hypertensive Patients." *Psychosomatic Medicine* 23 (1961): pp. 311-322.

Kaye, Ken. "Airline Seeks Ways to Ground Sky Rage." *Sun-Sentinel*, August 31, 1998.

Kesey, Ken. "Land of the Free, Home of the Bullets." *Rolling Stone.* July 9-23, 1998: pp. 51-56.

Kune, Gabriel, Susan Kune, Lyndsey Watson, and Claus Bahnson. "Personalitiy as a Risk Factor in Large Bowel Cancer: Data from the Melbourne Colorectal Cancer Study." *Psychological Medicine* 21/1 (1991): pp. 29-41.

Mann, A. H. "Psychiatric Morbidity and Hostility in Hypertension," *Psychological Medicine* 7 (1977): pp. 653-659.

Matshe, Thoko, "The Myths of Rape," Vol. 2. Woman Plus, 9-01-1997, pp. 3-4, Infonautics Corporation, 1998.

McGaha, Johnny. "Alcoholism and the Chemically Dependent Family: A Study of Adult Felons on Probation." *Journal of Offender Rehabilitation.* 193-4 (1993): pp. 57-69.

Morris, T. and S. Greer. "Psychological Atributes of Women Who Develop Breast Cancer: A Controlled Study." *Journal of Psychosomatic Research* 19 (1975): pp. 147-153.

Morrow, Lance. "Behavior Unspeakable." *Time*, (Feb. 22, 1993): p.48

Munhall, Patricia. "Women's Anger: A Phenomenological Perspective." *Health Care for Women International* 14/6 (1993): pp. 481-491.

Northam, Sarah, and Stephen D. Bluen. "Differential Correlates of Components of Type A Behavior." *South African Journal of Psychology* 24/3 (1994): pp. 131-137.

Palfai, Tibor P., and Kenneth Hart. "Anger Coping Styles and Perceived Social Support." *Journal of Social Psychology* 137/ 4 (1997): pp. 405-411.

Pang, Keum Young. "Hwabyung: The Construction of a Korean Popular Illness Among Korean Elderly Immigrant Women in the United States."

Culture, Medicine and Psychiatry 144 (Dec. 1990): pp. 495-512.

"Petition Drive Seeks Charges Against Killer's Friend." *The Las Vegas Sun,* August 22, 1998.

Rado, S. "The Problem of Melancholia." *The International Journal of Analysis* 9 (1928): pp. 420-438.

Richters, J. E., and R. Martinez. "The NIMH Community Violence Project 1: Children as Victims of and Witnesses to Violence." *Psychiatry* 56 (1993): pp. 7-21.

Schacter, J. "Pain, Fear and Anger in Hypertensives and Normotensives." *Psychosomatic Medicine* 19 (1957): pp. 17-29.

Scheir, M. F. and M. W. Bridges. "Person Variables and Health: Personality Predispositions and Acute Psychological States as Shared Determinants for Disease" (Review). *Psychosomatic Medicine* 57/3 (1995): pp. 255-268.

Swanson, Janice, Suzanne Dibble, and Carole Chenitz. "Clinical Features and Psychosocial Factors in Young Adults with Genital Herpes." *Image: The Journal of Nursing Scholarships* 27/1 (1995): pp. 16-22.

Talan, Jamie. "Sick or Stressed Out?" *Psychology Today* (July/August 1998): p. 18.

———. "Cardiac Consciousness-Raising." *Psychology Today* (July/August 1998): p. 18.

Temoshock, L., B. W. Heller, and R. W. Sagebriel. "The Relationship of Psychosocial Factors to Prognostic Indicators in Cutaneous Malignant Melanoma." *Journal of Psychosomatic Research* 29 (1985): pp. 135-153.

Thomas, Sandra P. "Relationships of Suppression to Blood Pressure. International Congress of Behavioral Medicine, Washington, District of Columbia, US." *Nursing Research* 466 (Nov.-Dec. 1997): pp. 324-330.

Wagner, Angie. "Casino Slaying Case Set for Trial." The Associated Press AP-NY-08-29-98, 1309 EDT.

Watson, Maggie, Steven Greer, Linda Rowden, Christine Gorman, et al. "Relationships Between Emotional Control, Adjustment to Cancer and Depression and Anxiety in Breast Cancer Patients." *Psychological Medicine* 21/1 (1991): pp. 51-57.

Williams, Redford B., et al. "Psychosocial Correlates of Job Strain in a Sample of Working Women." *Archives of General Psychiatry* 54 (1997): pp. 543-548.

INDEX

A

Abusive Partner: An Analysis of Domestic Battering, An, 194

accountability
    for emotional balance, 16–17
    rights without responsibilities, 249
    for violence, 133, 186–87, 198
    See also connection

ADD (attention deficit disorder), 13–14

Adler, Alfred, 109

adrenaline
    and depression, 101
    in "fight or flight," 25–30
    in rush of road rage, 143–44

adults and powerlessness, 80–82

Adventures of Little Tom Thumb, The, 12

African-American families, 120–21, 122

aggressor identification and lateral violence, 124–26

Akbar, Na'im, 120–21

America Online, 266

American Automobile Association (AAA) Foundation for Traffic Safety, 136, 138, 139–40, 145

American Psychiatric Association, 136

anger, healthy, 61, 62

anger, unhealthy
    definitions, 3–4
    myths about, 61–62
    rage vs., 4, 6
    See also depression; emotional balance, achieving; emotional balance, living in; killing; lateral violence; passive-aggressives; powerlessness; right controllers; road rage; sickness from anger; violence

anger-in (imploded anger), 33, 34, 37

anger-out (exploded anger), 33, 34, 37, 61

Anisman, H., 32

anonymity
    and right controllers, 164
    and road rage, 142–43

antidepressants, 271

anti-heroes and killing, 223

Applewhite, Marshall Herff, 166

Argument Culture, The (Tannen), 163

arguments vs. discussions, 162–64

Arrested Development, 178

Arrien, Angeles, 255

attention deficit disorder (ADD), 13–14

autogenocide. *See* lateral violence

B

Baer, P.E., 33

Bahnson, Claus, 32–33

Barefoot, J.C., 31–32

Beck, Melinda, 266

Belmont, Harold

   on connection, 18

   on evaluating balance, 262–65

   on trauma interventions, 108–9

Bettleheim, Bruno, 94–95

biochemistry of depression, 100–102

biofeedback, 35

Birnbaum, Jean H., 194

Blakelock, E.H., 33

blaming and Blame Game, 68–73

Block Watches, 254

blood pressure and anger, 33

Boal, Augusto, 132

body, listening to, 34–37

Bowlby, John, 89

boys

   and anger, 96

   socialization of and violence, 175–76

   See also children; family unit breakdown

Brave New World (Huxley), 85

C

cancer from anger, 32–33

Cannon, Walter, 31

Casino, 214

Chains and Images of Psychological Slavery (Akbar), 120

Changing Community (Walker), 15

Chavis, Reverend Benjamin, 265

childhood, blaming for violence, 189

Childhood's Future (Louv), 221

children

   emotional competency, learning, 7–8, 9, 12–13

   and killing, 210–12, 222–23, 225, 228–29

   lateral violence of, 121–23, 125–26

   powerlessness in, 76–79

   and self-worth, 87–88

   violence, views on, 231–43

   violence to, 179, 184

   youth and rebuilding communities, 256–57

   See also family unit breakdown

Cobain, Kurt, 223

college rape, 196, 206

communities
    concern for future of, 246–48
    rebuilding, 265–66
    violence, approach to, 204–8
    youth and rebuilding, 256–57
compassion and violence, 208
complaining, 66–68
conflict resolution, 229
connection
    celebrities for, 223
    for emotional balance, 18–20
    for passive-aggressives, 62
    for powerlessness, 81
    for sickness from anger, 40–42
    See also disconnection
control
    anger vs., 180, 183, 195–96, 201
    and rape, 195–96, 201
    and road rage, 146–47, 148
counseling
    for depression, 103–4, 108
    for domestic violence, 184
    for passive-aggressives, 60
    for rape, 201–2
    for rapists, 202–3
    for right controllers, 162
    for sickness from anger, 35–36
Cousins, Norman, 39
Cox, T., 32
Crime Victimization survey, 195
cultural identity elimination as
    lateral violence, 120–21
cumulative trauma and depression,
    94

D
Dahlstrom, W.G., 31–32
Davis, Angela, 116–17
De Puymege, Gerard, 169
delayed grief, 95
Department of Justice, 194
dependency
    and depression, 89
    financial, 119–20
    on government services, 250–53
    of right controllers, 171
    self-esteem and, 160–61, 162
depression, 83–113
    adrenaline, 101
    antidepressants for, 271
    assessment for, 103, 104–5
    and biochemistry, 100–102
    boys and anger, 96
    of children, 87–88
    cumulative trauma and, 94
    delayed grief, 95
    dependence, emotional, 89
    dopamine, 101, 102
    emotional landscape and,
        109–11
    exercise for, 104, 272
    girls and anger, 96
    grief vs. depression, 103
    group therapy for, 104
    internalization and, 88
    isolation and, 97, 103, 106
    learned helplessness, 97–100
    learning-style differences, 99
    life events and, 90–97
    light therapies for, 104
    loss and, 90–97

depression *(continued)*
  loss-sensitive, 92–93
  manic depression, 105
  mastery of, 111–13, 272–73
  of men, 96, 97
  mirroring for, 88, 107, 108–9
  monoamine oxidase (MAO)
    inhibitors for, 271–72
  moods and, 103
  neurotransmitters, 101, 102, 271
  norepinephrine, 101, 102, 271
  postpartum depression, 104
  prescription medications for,
    84–86, 269–73
  prevalence of, 84
  preventing and healing, 103–8
  professionals for, 103–4, 108
  Prozac for, 84–85
  repeated trauma and, 98, 99
  reuptake process, 101, 270, 271
  seasonal affective disorder
    (SAD), 105
  self-defeating thoughts and, 272
  self-hate and, 86–90
  serotonin, 101, 102, 271, 273
  serotonin syndrome and, 273
  shame-base of, 109–11
  St. John's wort for, 104, 272
  and stress cycle, 100–102
  suicide, 88, 96, 106–8
  support system for, 94–95
  synapses, 101
  trauma and, 90–97
  tricyclic medications for, 270
  uncontrollable events and, 98,
    99

  of veterans, 95–96
  of women, 96, 97
*Depression: How It Happens; How
  It's Healed* (Medina), 102
desensitization
  to killing, 212–15, 225
  to violence, 176–77
destructive anger, 61. *See also*
  anger, unhealthy
*Diagnostic and Statistical Manual of
  Mental Disorders,* 136
diet and behavior, 13, 14
disconnection
  and hate groups, 259
  and killing, 223–24, 229
  See also connection
discussions vs. arguments, 162–64
dividing and conquering as lateral
  violence, 123–24
domestic violence, 178–85, 205–6
Don't Drive When Driven, 146
dopamine, 101, 102
double-bind behavior, 45, 46,
  55–58
drivers as people, 147, 148–49, 150
drop-in centers, 206
Dyer, G., 213

E
education against lateral violence,
  131–32
elderly, violence to, 179
emotional abuse and violence, 183
emotional balance, achieving
  Block Watches for, 254
  communities, future of, 246–48

communities, rebuilding, 265–66
disconnection and hate groups, 259
emotional quadrant of balance, 262–63, 264
evaluation tool for, 262–65
Front Stoop Neighborhood Control for, 253–54
government, dependence on, 250–53
Internet chat rooms, 261
isolation and, 254
learned helplessness and, 250
mental quadrant of balance, 262, 264
Neighborhood Watches for, 254
physical quadrant of balance, 263, 264
politics and, 266
rights without responsibilities, 249
social services, dependence on, 250–53
spiritual quadrant of balance, 263, 264
standing up our relatives, 258–61
truth, learning to speak, 254–58
vision creation for, 267
youth response to, 256–57
See also depression; killing; lateral violence; passive-aggressives; powerlessness; right controllers; road rage; sickness from anger; violence

emotional balance, living in
accountability for, 16–17
anger definitions, 3–4
anger triggers, 17
attention deficit disorder (ADD), 13–14
awareness for, 19
children, learning emotional competency, 7–8, 9, 12–13
connection for, 18–20
defined, 19
diet and behavior, 13, 14
emotional competency, 6–10
families and, 5–6
guns and, 6
modeling for, 7–8, 9, 10–15
movies and, 5–6
operant conditioning techniques and, 13
rage vs. anger, 4, 6
"self-explore" vs. "other-blame," 17
technology effects on, 5–6, 9, 11, 15
television and, 11, 13, 14
video games and, 6
violence glorification, 5–6
working toward, 16–17
See also depression; killing; lateral violence; passive-aggressives; powerlessness; right controllers; road rage; sickness from anger; violence
emotional competency, 6–10
emotional landscape and depression, 109–11

emotional quadrant of balance, 262–63, 264

escort services against violence, 206

Esler, Gavin, 40

exercise
for depression, 104, 272
for powerlessness, 80–81

exploded anger (anger-out), 33, 34, 37, 61

extended family networks, 219–20, 229

F

Faces of Death, 215

family unit breakdown
and emotional balance, 5–6
and killing, 212, 219–24, 229
and lateral violence, 121–23
values, changing, 228–27
violence in family, 224–25

fanatics, 166–71

Farrakhan, Reverend Louis, 265

Faul, Stephanie, 136, 139

fear
and lateral violence, 129–30
and passive-aggressives, 61
and powerlessness, 79

"fight or flight," 25–30

financial dependence as lateral violence, 119–20

First Nations families, 122

Four-Fold Way: Walking the Paths of the Warrior, Healer & Visionary, The (Arrien), 255

Freire, Paulo, 130

Friedman, Meyer, 22

Front Stoop Neighborhood Control, 253–54

G

Gabriel, R., 213

gang
rape, 198–99, 207
violence as lateral violence, 131–32

Genovese, Kitty (murder of), 246

Ghetto Boys, 223

ghosts and sickness, 42

Gilligan, James, 175

girls and anger, 96. *See also* children; family unit breakdown

Goodfellas, 214

gossip as lateral violence, 128–29

Gottman, John, 194

government, dependence on, 250–53

Greer, S., 32

grief vs. depression, 103

Grossman, David, Lt. Col., 213–14, 217

Groth, A. Nicholas, 194, 200–201

group blaming, 75

guns
control laws for, 228
and emotional balance, 6
killing with, 217–19
and road rage, 150
violence using, 187

H

Harburg, E., 33

Haynal, Aldous, 169

healthy anger, 61, 62
heart disease from anger, 31–32
Hiroshima, 214
Hitler, Adolf, 166
horizontal violence. *See* lateral
    violence
hot lines, 205
humor for sickness, 38–40
Hunt, Steven, 101
Huxley, Aldous, 85
Hwabyung (fire illness), 33–34

I
*I Don't Want to Talk About It
    (Real)*, 96
imploded anger (anger-in), 33,
    34, 37
Independence Day, 214
internalization and depression, 88
Internet chat rooms and
    connection, 261
invisibility and road rage, 142–43
Irwin, J., 32
isolation
    and depression, 97, 103, 106
    and emotional balance, 254
    and violence, 205

J
Jacobson, Neil, 194
Jensen, Jean, 41
Jerry Springer Show, The, 11, 214
Jewish families, 122
Jones, Jim, 166
journaling for sickness, 36–37

K
Kaplan, S., 33
Kesey, Ken, 18
killing, 209–29
    anti-heroes and, 223
    celebrities for connection, 223
    children and, 210–12, 222–23,
        225, 228–29
    conflict resolution, healthy, 229
    convictions that lead to, 226–27
    desensitization to, 212–15, 225
    disconnection and, 223–24, 229
    extended family networks,
        219–20, 229
    family unit breakdown and,
        212, 219–24, 229
    family values, changing, 228–27
    family violence, 224–25
    gun control laws and, 228
    guns and, 217–19
    latchkey kids and, 220
    modeling importance, 223
    in movies, 212, 213–14, 215, 228
    in music, 212, 228
    operant conditioning
        techniques and, 215–17
    popular culture and, 212
    prevention programs for, 229
    psychopathy and, 221
    role models, healthy, 229
    solutions to, 227–29
    teachers, training, 228–29
    on television, 212, 214, 228
    in videos, 212, 215, 228
    violence glorification, laws
        against, 228

killing *(continued)*
   weapons and, 217–19
   at Westside Middle School,
     217–18, 221–23
Koresh, David, 166
Kune, Gabriel and Susan, 32–33

L
latchkey kids and killing, 220
lateral violence, 115–34
   accountability for, 133
   of African-Americans, 120–21,
     122
   aggression release, 128–29
   aggressor identification, 124–26
   of children, 121–23, 125–26
   cultural identity elimination as,
     120–21
   defined, 117–18
   development of, 124–31
   dividing and conquering as,
     123–24
   education against, 131–32
   family unit breakdown and,
     121–23
   fear of change and choice,
     129–30
   financial dependence as, 119–20
   of First Nations children, 122
   gang violence as, 131–32
   gossip as, 128–29
   of Jewish population, 122
   leadership, undermining as, 123
   learned helplessness and,
     127–28

   learned optimism against,
     133–34
   of Native Americans, 122
   of nurses, 134
   oppression and, 118–24
   oppressor tactics
     internalization, 126–27
   participation, refusal, 131
   personalizing and, 133
   political infighting as, 126
   of prisoners of war, 130
   self-hate, 124–31
   stereotyping as, 119
   stopping, 131–34
   symptoms of, 117
   Theater of the Oppressed, 132
   welfare system and, 119–20
   of women by men, 119
   zero tolerance for, 134
laws
   for domestic violence, 184
   for gun control, 228
   against violence glorification,
     228
leadership, undermining as lateral
   violence, 123
learned behavior, violence as,
   175–78
learned helplessness
   and depression, 97–100
   and emotional balance, 250
   and lateral violence, 127–28
learned optimism against lateral
   violence, 133–34
learning-style differences and
   depression, 99

Lefkowitz, Bernard, 176
Leo, John, 249
Lerner, Harriet, 156
Lerner, Michael, 144–45
life events and depression, 90–97
light therapies for depression, 104
loss and depression, 90–97
loss-sensitive, 92–93
Louv, Richard, 221

M
manic depression, 105
Mann, A.H., 33
MAO (monoamine oxidase)
    inhibitors, 271–72
Marshall, S.L.A., 213
Matshe, Thoko, 196
media, violence in, 176–77, 178.
    See also movies; music;
        television; videos
Medina, John, 102
men
    as abusers, 187–88
    and depression, 96, 97
    rape of, 190–201
    violence to, 179, 199–201
*Men Who Rape: The Psychology of
    the Offender* (Groth and
        Birnbaum), 194, 200
Menace to Society, 214
mental health professionals and
    denial of violence, 190–92
mental quadrant of balance, 262,
    264
Miller, Alice, 168–69
Million Man March, 265

Minnesota Multiphasic Personality
    Inventory (MMPI), 31–32
mirroring and depression, 88, 107,
    108–9
mistakes
    and love, 161
    and powerlessness, 82
MMPI (Minnesota Multiphasic
    Personality Inventory), 31–32
modeling importance
    and killing, 223
    and powerlessness, 77–78
    role models, healthy, 229
    in society, 10–15
    and violence, 179, 185, 188, 205
Molnar, Miklos, 169
monoamine oxidase (MAO)
    inhibitors, 271–72
moods and depression, 103
moral and righteous anger, 165–69
Morris, T., 32
movies
    and emotional balance, 5–6
    killing in, 212, 213–14, 215, 228
    violence in, 178
music
    killing in, 212, 228
    violence in, 177
Myths of Rape, The (Matshe), 196

N
narcissists, 166–67
National Institute of Mental
    Health, 196
Native American families, 122
Neibuhr, Reinhold, 148

Neighborhood Watches, 254
Nerenberg, Arnold, 136
neurotransmitters, 101, 102, 271
Newsweek magazine, 222–23
norepinephrine, 101, 102, 271
Northern Exposure, 260
"Now I've Got You" game, 67, 74
nurses and lateral violence, 134

O

obsessive relationships, 160
On Killing: The Psychological Cost of Learning to Kill in War and Society (Grossman), 213
operant conditioning techniques, 13, 177, 215–17
oppression and lateral violence, 118–24
organ abnormalities from anger, 31
"other-blame" vs. "self-explore," 17
Our Guys (Lefkowitz), 176

P

partners who abuse, 185–89
passive-aggressives, 43–62
    anger, myths about, 61–62
    anger-out (exploded anger), 61
    being late behavior of, 55–56
    caretaking and, 54, 55
    changing cycle of, 60–62
    connection for, 62
    counseling for, 60
    dealing with behavior of, 53–60
    defined, 45
    destructive anger, 61
    double-bind behaviors of, 45, 46, 55–58
    fear of anger and, 61
    gossip, 128–29
    healthy anger, 61, 62
    messages (unclear) of, 57
    pattern of, 52
    personalizing and, 59–60
    picking up after oneself behavior of, 58
    promises (broken) of, 57
    recognizing, 55–58
    reverse puppets, 51, 61
    triggers for, 46–47
perfection for love, 159–60
personalizing
    and lateral violence, 133
    and passive-aggressives, 59–60
    and powerlessness, 74
physical quadrant of balance, 263, 264
physiological effects of anger, 25–30, 100–102
Picket Fences, 260
Pipher, Mary, 15
political infighting as lateral violence, 126
politics and emotional balance, 266
postpartum depression, 104
post-traumatic stress, 202
power
    anger vs., 180, 183, 195–96, 201
    feelings of road rage, 144–45
powerlessness, 63–82
    adults with, 80–82

blaming and Blame Game, 68–73
children with, 76–79
complaining, 66–68
connection for, 81
dealing with behavior of, 73–76
discipline for, 79
exercise for, 80–81
fear and, 79
group blaming, 75
listening and, 74
mistakes and, 82
modeling importance, 77–78
"Now I've Got You" game, 67, 74
personalizing and, 74
and road rage, 149
solution focus for, 81
"Twinkie Defense," 71
wants, stating clearly, 80
whining, 65–66
prescription medications for depression, 84–86, 269–73
prevention programs for killing, 229
prison rape, 200
prisoners of war and lateral violence, 130
Prozac, 84–85
psychopathy and killing, 221

R
Rado, S., 86
rage vs. anger, 4, 6
rape, 194–203, 206–7
Real, Terrence, 96

Reclaiming Your Life (Jensen), 41–42
"reflection," 33
repeated trauma and depression, 98, 99
resentments, collecting, 154–55
Reservoir Dogs, 214
reuptake process, 101, 270, 271
reverse puppets, 51, 61
right controllers, 151–71
anonymity and, 164
arguments vs. discussions, 162–64
changing cycle of, 160–62
changing others, 161–62
characteristics of, 159–60
convincing others of your goodness, 160
counseling for, 162
dependency and, 171
fanatics, 166–71
followers of fanatics, 169–71
issues, underlying, 155–59
mistakes and love, 161
moral and righteous anger, 165–69
narcissists, 166–67
obsessive relationships, 160
perfection for love, 159–60
resentments, collecting, 154–55
self-esteem and dependence, 160–61, 162
silence, using, 155
technology and, 164
them vs. us, 162–64
rights without responsibilities, 249

road rage, 135–50
   adrenaline rush of, 143–44
   anger, expressing appropriately
     and, 146
   anonymous other and, 142–43
   built-up anger and, 141
road rage (continued)
   changing cycle of, 145–49
   control and, 146–47, 148
   defined, 136
   development of, 140–43
   drivers as people, 147, 148–49,
     150
   help, seeking, 150
   invisible belief and, 142–43
   locking doors and, 150
   power feelings of, 144–45
   powerlessness and, 149
   provocation, reacting to, 150
   reasons for, 143–45
   Serenity Prayer for, 148
   space between drivers, 150
   stress, coping with, 147–48
   technology and, 137–38
   triggers for, 146, 147–48
   victims of, 149–50
   weapons and, 150
Robson, Ruthann, 126–27
role models, healthy, 229.
   See also modeling importance
Roper, P.J., 33
Rosenman, Ray, 22, 31
Roy, Maria, 189, 194

S
SAD (seasonal affective disorder),
   105
safe homes, 205
safety plan, establishing, 185
same-sex partners, violence to,
   179–80
Schacter, J., 33
screening for violence, 192–94
seasonal affective disorder (SAD),
   105
self-defeating thoughts and
   depression, 272
self-esteem and dependence,
   160–61, 162
"self-explore" vs. "other-blame," 17
self-hate
   and depression, 86–90
   and lateral violence, 124–31
Seligman, Martin, 98, 99, 111
Serenity Prayer, 148
serotonin, 101, 102, 271, 273
serotonin syndrome, 273
sexual assault, 194–203, 206–7
shame-base of depression, 109–11
Shelter of Each Other, The (Pipher),
   15
Shulman, Benard, 109
sickness from anger, 21–42
   anger-in (imploded anger),
     33, 34, 37
   anger-out (exploded anger),
     33, 34, 37
   biofeedback for, 35
   blood pressure and, 33
   body, listening to, 34–37

cancer, 32–33
connection for, 40–42
doctors for, 35–36
"fight or flight," 25–30
ghosts and, 42
heart disease, 31–32
humor for, 38–40
Hwabyung (fire illness), 33–34
journaling for, 36–37 organ
    abnormalities, 31
physiological effects of, 25–30,
    100–102
"reflection," 33
solutions for, 34–40
studies on, 31–34
triggers for, 37–40
Type A personalities, 22–23
Type C personalities, 32
silence and right controllers, 155
Skekelle, 31
Skinner, B.F., 215
Snoop Doggy Dogg, 177, 223
social services, dependence on,
    250–53
South Park, 12, 214
spiritual quadrant of balance, 263,
    264
St. John's wort, 104, 272
standing up our relatives, 258–61
stereotyping as lateral violence, 119
stress and driving, 147–48
substance abuse and violence, 186
suicide, 88, 96, 106–8
survival kits, 184
synapses and depression, 101

T
Tannen, Deborah, 163, 164
teacher training to identify
    violence, 228–29
technology impact
    on emotional balance, 5–6, 9,
        11, 15
    on right controllers, 164
    on road rage, 137–38
television
    and emotional balance, 11, 13,
        14
    killing on, 212, 214, 228
    violence on, 178
Temoshock, L., 32
Theater of the Oppressed, 132
them vs. us, 162–64
Time magazine, 199
trauma and depression, 90–97
tricyclic medications, 270
triggers
    defined, 17
    for passive-aggressives, 46–47
    for road rage, 146, 147–48
    for sickness, 37–40
truth, learning to speak, 254–58
"Twinkie Defense," 71
Type A personalities, 22–23
Type C personalities, 32

U
uncontrollable events and
    depression, 98, 99
unhealthy anger. See anger,
    unhealthy

United States of Anger, The (Esler), 40

University of Rhode Island, 249

Untouched Key, The (Miller), 168

V

veterans and depression, 95–96

victims
    of domestic violence, 183–85

victims *(continued)*
    of rape, 201–2
    of road rage, 149–50

videos
    and emotional balance, 6
    killing in, 212, 215, 228
    violence in, 178

violence, 173–208
    accountability for, 186–87, 198
    boys' socialization and, 175–76
    childhood, blaming for, 189
    to children, 179, 184
    children's views of, 231–43
    college rape, 196, 206
    community approach to, 204–8
    compassion and, 208
    desensitization to, 176–77
    domestic violence, 178–85, 205–6
    drop-in centers for, 206
    to elderly, 179
    emotional abuse and, 183
    escort services against, 206
    gang rape, 198–99, 207
    glorification of, 5–6, 228
    hot lines for, 205
    isolation and, 205

    laws against domestic violence, 184
    laws against glorification, 228
    as learned behavior, 175–78
    in media, 176–77, 178
    to men, 179, 199–201
    men, rape of, 190–201
    men abusers, 187–88
    mental health professionals and, 190–92
    modeling importance, 179, 185, 188, 205
    in movies, 178
    in music, 177
    networks, supportive, 184
    operant conditioning techniques and, 177
    partners who abuse, 185–89
    personal impact, lacking, 177
    post-traumatic stress of, 202
    power and control vs. anger, 180, 183, 195–96, 201
    prison rape, 200
    rape, 194–203, 206–7
    rapists, seeking help, 202–3
    safe homes for, 205
    safety plan, establishing, 185
    to same-sex partners, 179–80
    self-love and, 189
    senseless violence, exposure to, 176
    skilled screening, importance of, 192–94
    substance abuse and, 186
    survival kits, 184
    in television, 178

victims of domestic violence,
183–85
victims of rape, 201–2
in video games, 178
war and rape, 199
"We Care" task forces for, 207
weapons and, 187
witnessing of, 180
to women, 179, 194–99
women, rape of, 194–99
vision creation for emotional
balance, 267

W
Walker, Scott, 15
war and rape, 199
Watson, Lyndsey, 32–33
"We Care" task forces, 207
weapons
and emotional balance, 6
gun control laws, 228
killing with, 217–19
and road rage, 150
violence using, 187
welfare system and lateral violence,
119–20
Westside Middle School killings,
217–18, 221–23
*When Men Batter Women: New
Insights into Ending Abusive
Relationships, The* (Jacobson
and Gottman), 194
whining, 65–66
Williams, R.D., 31–32
Willis, David K., 138
witnessing of violence, 180

women
and depression, 96, 97
lateral violence to, 119
rape of, 194–99
violence to, 179, 194–99

Y
youth response to communities
rebuilding, 256–57.
See also children; family unit
breakdown

New!

#1 New York Times **BESTSELLING AUTHORS**

Jack Canfield
Mark Victor Hansen
Mark & Chrissy Donnelly
and
Barbara De Angelis, Ph.D.

Chicken Soup for the Couple's Soul

With Stories By:
Paul Reiser
Marianne Williamson
Deepak Chopra
George Burns
Joan Wester Anderson
Charlton Heston
And Many More

Inspirational Stories About
Love and Relationships

Bestselling author Barbara De Angelis teams up as a coauthor for this collection of stories about how people were transformed when they discovered true love. With chapters on intimacy, commitment, understanding and overcoming obstacles, couples and singles alike will look to this book as a source of love and inspiration for Valentine's Day and throughout the entire year.

Code 6463, quality softcover, $12.95